TODAY
IS YOUR **BEST** DAY

DISCOVERING GOD'S BEST FOR YOU

TODAY
IS YOUR **BEST** DAY

Roy Lessin

BARBOUR
PUBLISHING

Cover design by Kirk DouPonce, DogEaredDesign.com

Published by Barbour Publishing, Inc., P.O. Box 719, Uhrichsville, Ohio 44683
www.barbourbooks.com

Our mission is to publish and distribute inspirational products offering exceptional value and biblical encouragement to the masses.

ecpa Member of the
Evangelical Christian
Publishers Association

Printed in China.

5 4 3 2 1

CONTENTS

This book is dedicated to the staff of Bethany College of Missions (Bethany Fellowship 1961–64), whose guidance, wisdom, instruction, and love planted the seeds of God's Kingdom that have grown within me over the past forty years.

This book is written to those who have received Jesus Christ by faith as their Lord and Savior, and who have committed their lives to walk daily with Him.

If you have never turned your life over to Jesus Christ, and do not know the meaning of forgiveness for your sins, I have written the following section just for you. In this section you will discover how to receive Jesus Christ as your very own.

Today Is Your Best Day
Because of Salvation

For God says, "At just the right time, I heard you. On the day of salvation, I helped you." Indeed, God is ready to help you right now. Today is the day of salvation.

2 CORINTHIANS 6:2 NLT

Salvation means that God has made everything that is right, true, loving, and good available to you through His Son, Jesus Christ. Salvation is God's good news to your heart, your life, and your future.

Salvation means a new life; victory and deliverance from the pain and judgment of sin; freedom from the bondage of Satan and the powers of darkness; peace, joy, and fellowship with God. It means that God's will has become your will; that God's plans are your plans; that God's blessings are your blessings.

Salvation means that God has not said to you, "I want you to work your way to Me. I want you to try to save yourself by being good." Instead, God has said to you, "You don't have to work your way to Me, because I have come to you. I sent My Son to earth to die for you, be buried for you, and rise from the dead for you. He shed His blood on the cross so that your sins can be forgiven."

Salvation is God's free gift to you because of His grace and mercy. You cannot earn it. Salvation can only be received by faith alone in Jesus Christ.

Salvation also brings you the hope of eternal life. Salvation means that you will not be lost, or have to pay the penalty for your sins, because Jesus has paid that penalty by dying in your place. It means that you have escaped eternal condemnation and separation from God, and will have a home with Him in heaven forever.

You can receive the gift of Salvation at this very moment. Turn now from your sins, ask God to forgive you, and open your heart to Jesus Christ. By faith, receive Him as your Lord and Savior. Ask Jesus to save you this very moment.

As you do, today will truly be your best day!

It is my prayer that God will use *Today Is Your Best Day* to bless, encourage, and enrich your life.

ROY LESSIN

> *This is the day which the LORD hath made;*
> *we will rejoice and be glad in it.*
> PSALM 118:24 KJV

Today is Your Best Day

In God we boast all day long, and praise Your name forever.
PSALM 44:8 NKJV

If you are in Jesus Christ and your heart is committed to God's plan for your life, it means that today is your best day. It's not your best day because you feel like it is, or because you pretend that it is. It is not your best day because everything is going perfectly, or because you are living in ideal circumstances. It is not your best day because you are in optimum health, or because everything is going your way.

Here are four reasons why today is your best day.

1. Today is your best day because you are here. God has placed you in this moment of time for a purpose, and the things that happen to you today will be an unfolding of that purpose.

2. What happened to you yesterday, however easy or difficult, was used by God to help prepare

you for what He has for you today.

3. God will use what happens today to prepare you for what He has for you in future days.

4. God has used your past and worked it all together for the good, and He will use this day to add to the good that He has already worked on your behalf.

Today is your best day because you can grow a little more in your faith, a little more in your maturity, and a little more in your intimacy with Jesus. Today you can take another step higher as He takes you from glory to glory; take another step deeper as you grow in His love; take another step farther as you obediently walk with Him. Today is your best day because it has brought you one day closer to the coming of the Lord.

You may be going through a very difficult time today, but that does not mean this is your worst day. God will use the difficulty to produce precious things within you that you will treasure in days to come. There may be pressures in your day, but God uses pressure to form diamonds. There may be a fiery trial in your day, but God uses fire to purify gold. There may be an irritant in your day, but God uses irritants to create pearls. If you are in need of comfort today, God will bring His comfort to you, and the comfort you receive will help you comfort someone tomorrow.

Corrie ten Boom once said, "God doesn't have problems, He only has plans." God doesn't make bad days for you and good days for you. God makes each day fit perfectly into His plans for you. He made this day so you could glorify Him. He made this day so that He could draw you closer to His heart. He made this day so that you could see your life from faith's point of view.

Today Is Your Best Day

Because of Faith (Part 1)

For therein is the righteousness of God revealed from faith to faith: as it is written, The just shall live by faith.
ROMANS 1:17 KJV

There are two ways that we can walk through a day. One is to walk by sight and the other is to walk by faith. If we walk by sight we can easily become discouraged, disappointed, and downhearted. To walk by sight means to evaluate our day by what we see with our eyes, hear with our ears, and know in our minds. To walk by sight means to allow the "reality" around us to impact our thoughts, our motivation, and our emotions.

A large percentage of the "walk by sight" information that influences us in our day is negative. Anyone who tunes in to the evening news or reads a newspaper finds very little that brings a smile. When we walk by sight we can allow anything or anyone to influence the kind of day we are having—the weather, the traffic, the long line at the checkout stand, a problem with our computer, a drop of ketchup on our shirt, or a leaky faucet under the kitchen sink.

To walk by faith means to walk in a different kind of reality. The Bible tells us that there are two realities (2 Corinthians 4:17–18). One reality is what is seen; the other reality is what is unseen. There are two realities because there are two worlds. One is the physical world; the other is the spiritual world. The physical world is the temporary world; the spiritual world is the eternal world.

Today, as a believer and a follower of Jesus Christ, you live in both worlds. Through your senses you connect with the physical world around you, and with your heart and spirit you connect with the spiritual world within you. Your spiritual reality is not based upon wishful thinking or some unknown mystic influence, but upon the truth of God's Word and the presence of the Holy Spirit who lives in you.

As you walk through this day in both worlds, God wants you to live by faith and not by sight.

> *Faith sees what your physical eyes can never see; Faith knows what your natural mind can never comprehend; Faith possesses what your physical arms can never hold. Faith says "yes" to everything God declares to be true; Faith stands upon everything God says is certain, it leans upon everything God says is unmovable, and it counts upon everything God says will come to pass.*

Today Is Your Best Day

Because of Faith (Part 2)

What is faith? It is the confident assurance that what we hope for is going to happen. It is the evidence of things we cannot yet see. . . . So, you see, it is impossible to please God without faith. Anyone who wants to come to him must believe that there is a God and that he rewards those who sincerely seek him.

HEBREWS 11:1, 6 NLT

Your faith in God today is your lifeline to His heartbeat. Faith is the hand that reaches up and takes hold of God's promises and gathers in the spiritual treasures that are found in Christ. Faith sees the sunshine of God's face, even when there are dark clouds all around.

It is quite an experience the first time someone flies in a plane. The sky may be covered with dark clouds, but soon after takeoff, the plane breaks through the clouds. The passenger quickly discovers that the sky is still blue and the sun is still shining, even though things look quite different below.

What things are possible for you today through faith? All things are possible, because your faith is in the God who knows no impossibilities.

- *When the things that you are experiencing don't make sense, faith says, "God knows what He is doing."*
- *When your resources don't match your need, faith says, "God is my provider."*
- *When you are fearful to take the next step, faith says, "God will not fail me."*
- *When you're not sure what to do next, faith says, "God will guide me."*
- *When you are in a situation that seems impossible, faith says, "Nothing is too hard for the Lord."*

When I was a new Christian living in Southern California, I applied to a Bible school in the Midwest. The school accepted my application. Along with the application, the school sent me the date that they wanted me to arrive and start my classes. I bought a plane ticket and started getting things in order. The night before my flight, the local weather forecast reported that the area would be covered with thick fog in the morning. My flight was scheduled to leave early that morning. Instead of worrying about it, I got on my knees and asked the Lord to lift the fog. By faith, I knew that God would answer that prayer. I told the person who was taking me to the airport that God would lift the fog, and that my flight would not be canceled. The next morning we headed out to the airport under clear skies.

Where will your faith journey with God lead you today? Whatever the step may be, wherever the path may lead, you can be certain that your obedience of faith will always bring you into His best.

Today Is Your Best Day

Because of Jesus' Name

*Wherefore God also hath highly exalted him, and given him a
name which is above every name: That at the name of Jesus
every knee should bow, of things in heaven, and things
in earth, and things under the earth.*

PHILIPPIANS 2:9–10 KJV

Jesus' name is above every name. His name is so great
that the Bible gives Him many other names to help us
understand how mighty He truly is. Every name that
Jesus bears and everything that Jesus is, He is for you. As you
go through this day consider His glorious names, and the
impact they have upon your life.

- *The Last Adam:* Through His obedience He
  came to restore to you everything that the first
  Adam lost through his disobedience.
- *The Advocate:* He is your defending attorney in
  the courtrooms of heaven.

- *Almighty:* He knows no limits to what He can do for you because He is without limitation.
- *Alpha:* He is the first word in every issue that concerns you.
- *Omega:* He is the final word in every issue that concerns you.
- *Amen:* He is the "so be it" to all He directs you to do.
- *Anointed:* He is the One God has chosen to be your all in all.
- *Apostle:* He is the One who established you and upon whom the foundation of your faith is built.
- *Author:* He is writing every chapter of your life and is preparing future editions.
- *Beloved:* He brings you the Father's heart.
- *Bishop:* He watches over your soul.
- *Bread of Life:* He nurtures and sustains you.
- *Bridegroom:* He's preparing you for His wedding day.
- *Bright Morning Star:* He is the bright spot in your day.
- *Captain:* He is charting your course and guiding your rudder.
- *Carpenter:* He is preparing a place for you in His Father's house.

- *Chief Shepherd:* He is leading you to still waters and quiet resting places.
- *Christ:* He is the Lord of your life.
- *Cornerstone:* He is the One you are building your life upon.
- *Dayspring from on High:* He brings new hope to every morning.
- *Deliverer:* He is the One who sets you free from the bondage of sin.
- *Emmanuel:* He is God with you.
- *Express Image of God:* He allows you to see the beauty of the Father's face.
- *High Priest:* He is praying for you and standing before God on your behalf.
- *Holy One:* He is your purity.
- *Jesus:* He is your Savior.
- *Lamb of God:* He is your sacrifice.
- *Master:* He is in control.
- *Messiah:* He is the God of Abraham, Isaac, and Jacob—and He is your God.
- *Passover:* He has provided your redemption.
- *Propitiation:* He has made atonement for you.
- *Rabbi:* He is your teacher.
- *Refuge:* He is your hiding place.
- *Resurrection:* He is your eternal hope.
- *Vine:* He makes you fruitful.

- *Wonderful:* He is the One who is worthy of all your worship.
- *Way:* He is the pathway and the destination of your day.

Today Is Your Best Day

Because You Are in Christ

God alone made it possible for you to be in Christ Jesus.
For our benefit God made Christ to be wisdom itself.
He is the one who made us acceptable to God.
He made us pure and holy, and he gave
himself to purchase our freedom.

1 CORINTHIANS 1:30 NLT

Different people use different measurements to evaluate their day. A salesman may land a big account and call it his best day. An athlete may break a record in his sport and call it his best day. A woman may marry the man of her dreams and call it her best day. A writer may have her first book published and call it her best day.

As a child of God, however, today is your best day because you are in Christ. You may be a salesman who landed a big account today, or you may have made no sale at all. Your best day is not founded in what you've accomplished, but in who you are in Christ.

Being in Christ means that He is the atmosphere in which you live your day.

I was recently in a large conference room for a staff meeting. Because I was *in* the room, the atmosphere of the room had an influence upon me. The room had padded chairs to sit upon. The lighting in the room was soft and inviting. The colors on the walls were pleasing to the eye. Best of all, the room was air-conditioned, making everyone inside feel comfortable, even though it was hot outside.

Because you are *in* Christ, everything that is true about Christ will have an impact upon you. It is in Him that you live and move and have your being. As you go through this day, consider all that is yours because you are in Christ.

- *You stand before God with your past forgiven and forgotten.*
- *Your life is under His ownership and watch-care.*
- *You have been brought into union and fellowship with God.*
- *You have no cloud of condemnation hanging over your head.*
- *You are no longer a slave to the sins that once had you bound.*
- *You are covered by the love of God from every direction.*
- *You are God's child and a part of God's family of believers.*
- *You have been set apart for God's special purpose.*
- *You can see life with a heavenly point of view.*

- *You are in God's strong hands.*
- *You travel on paths of victory as you walk with your hand in His.*
- *You have a new calling, a new purpose, and a new direction.*
- *You overflow with spiritual blessings.*
- *You live under and in the authority of Jesus.*
- *You are showered with grace and kindness.*
- *You are God's masterpiece in the making.*
- *You have a relationship with Jesus that will never end.*
- *You can go through this day clothed with the righteousness of Christ.*

Today Is Your Best Day

Because Christ Is in You

*For it has pleased God to tell his people that the riches and glory
of Christ are for you Gentiles, too. For this is the secret:
Christ lives in you, and this is your assurance that
you will share in his glory.*
COLOSSIANS 1:27 NLT

One of the glorious things about the Christian life is that God not only places you in Christ, but Christ also comes to live in you. It is one thing to be standing in a river and enjoy its benefits as it washes and refreshes you; it is another thing to have the river in you as a result of drinking from its waters. When the river is in you, you receive benefits that differ from the benefits you receive when you are standing in the river. The water now becomes a part of your being as it nourishes your body and supplies it with the minerals it needs to survive.

Being in Christ means that you receive the benefits of all that He has done for you through His death, burial, resurrection, and ascension; Christ being in you means that you receive the benefits of His presence, His character, and His nature within you.

- *Being in Christ changes your position before God; Christ being in you changes the inward condition of your heart.*
- *Being in Christ brings you into heavenly realities; Christ being in you brings heavenly realities into your earthly walk.*
- *Being in Christ opens your eyes to the beauty of God's love; Christ being in you floods your heart with that same love.*
- *Being in Christ allows you to see what God wants you to become; Christ being in you means that you can become what God wants you to be.*

Christ in you means that He has begun a good work in you, that He will sustain the work He has begun, and that He will complete the work He has begun. Christ in you means that He does the work of conforming you to His image, that He is the Master Craftsman who is shaping your life, and that He is the True Vine who is producing the good fruit of eternal life within you. Christ in you means that His strength is your strength, His peace is your peace, His power is your power, and His victory is your victory.

God is not asking you to act like Jesus today. He is asking you to surrender to Jesus and trust Him completely to be your life today. Letting Jesus be Jesus in you and through you makes this your best day. Trying to act like Jesus will only wear you down and tire you out. Expecting your efforts to be fruitful would be like cutting a branch off an apple tree and expecting it to grow apples. The reason an apple tree grows apples is because everything in an apple tree is designed for apples—within the sap is the life of every apple.

Think of this one truth as you go through this day: "Everything that is good, wise, loving, righteous, true, wonderful, kind, and caring is in Jesus Christ, and Jesus Christ is living His life in me."

Today Is Your Best Day

Because of Your Heavenly Calling

I strain to reach the end of the race and receive the prize for which God, through Christ Jesus, is calling us up to heaven.

PHILIPPIANS 3:14 NLT

Imagine that one day a skilled mountain climber reads an article about a new mountain peak that had been conquered. The author of the article says that in all his years of climbing, he had never seen a view as beautiful as the one from the summit of this new mountain. The author goes on to say that it was the most difficult climb he had ever made, but that the reward far outweighed the effort.

In response to the article, the reader thinks, "I must see this view. I will begin planning my climb immediately."

It takes the climber some time to pull together all the resources he needs to make the journey. He even manages to persuade a climbing buddy to make the trip with him. Six months later, the climber and his buddy arrive at their destination. Within a few days, the man's climbing buddy becomes ill and is unable to make the final ascent to the mountain's peak. Leaving his buddy behind, the climber sets out alone. He tells his buddy that he will keep in daily radio contact with him and report back on his progress.

When the climber radios in his first report he says, "I had a great day, and although the climb was slow and difficult, I climbed eight hundred feet up the slope."

The next day the climber radios in and reports that the climb was slow and difficult, but that he had climbed another thousand feet. On the third day the climber radios his buddy and says, "The climb is still difficult, but today was my best day. I climbed five hundred feet."

"How can you consider today to be your best day on the mountain if you have climbed less than you did on the other two days?"

The climber replies, "I didn't mean that this is my best day in comparison to how far I climbed on the other two days. This is my best day because I am now five hundred feet closer than I've ever been before to reaching the summit, and seeing that glorious view."

The apostle Paul was a remarkable man with an amazing focus on where he was and where he was going. There was nothing Paul faced that prevented him from daily moving onward toward his heavenly calling in Christ. Problems didn't deter him, trials didn't discourage him, persecution didn't defeat him, and hardships didn't weigh him down. Paul wasn't looking back, turning back, or going back to anything in his past. He didn't sit around counting the miles he had traveled or the distance he had come, but he pressed forward with his eyes on the summit of God's call and the glorious view of the heavenly things that awaited him.

There is a heavenly call of God upon you today. A call for you to move on and press on toward all that He has prepared for you. Yesterday's progress is all behind you. Your best day is today, and whether you take a small step forward or a giant leap, this day will move you closer than you have ever been before.

Today Is Your Best Day

Because of Mercy, Peace, and Love

May you receive more and more of God's mercy, peace, and love.
JUDE 1:2 NLT

What a day this is! You have never gone this way before. Today may be the start of an anticipated vacation, the day of a planned event, or it may be a normal day spent around the house or at the office. What you have planned for today is not what makes it meaningful. What makes your day meaningful is that God is in it.

He was in it when you first opened your eyes. He has sustained you through the night, greeted you with new mercies at morning's light, given you the breath of life, and promised to direct your steps until day's end.

Because of God's mercies you can follow Him with all of your heart today, assured that there is nothing being held over your head to condemn you; you can take each step today with a quiet heart knowing that His peace keeps you steady and sure; you can move ahead today with great confidence of faith knowing His love keeps you close to His heart, mindful of His promises, and confident of His care. God's mercies declare that you are covered in His compassion; His peace proclaims that you are renewed in His rest; His love heralds that you are bathed in His blessings of joy.

Are you tired or weary today? Allow God to renew you with His strength. Are you discouraged or downhearted? Allow God to lift you with His love. Are you carrying a burden of sin? Allow God's mercies to restore you. Are you in need of reassurance? Allow God to hold you in His embrace. Are you in need of healing? Allow God to mend you with His touch.

Today, you are His child and He is your Father—you belong to Him and He belongs to you; He matters to you and you matter to Him; you are committed to Him and He is committed to you. Today, there is mercy, there is peace, and there is love for your faith to receive.

Today Is Your Best Day

Because of the Kingdom of God

For the Kingdom of God is not just fancy talk;
it is living by God's power.
1 CORINTHIANS 4:20 NLT

The Kingdom of God makes all the difference in you and in your day because you are a part of it. There is no kingdom, rule, or authority that is greater than God's Kingdom. The Kingdom of God is all about the reign of Jesus Christ in your life. Jesus is the King of the Kingdom, and every benefit of the Kingdom is yours because you have the King ruling your life.

Jesus reigns and rules over everything that He has destroyed, over everything He has defeated, and over everything He has conquered. Jesus is the triumphant King, the mighty Warrior, and the risen Lord. He faced the onslaughts of Satan's attacks and crushed them; He faced the temptations of sin and overcame them; He faced the grip of death and triumphed over it. Today, Jesus is your authority over the kingdom of darkness, He is your deliverer over the power of sin, and He is your victory over the fear of death.

Jesus' Kingdom within you is unshakable, indestructible, and impenetrable. Nothing can come against it and prevail; nothing can challenge it and win; nothing can defy it and overcome. The Kingdom of God means that you do not have to live this day in your own strength, but by Jesus' power; not in your own efforts, but in Jesus' finished work; not in your own abilities, but in Jesus' endless resources.

- *If you are facing temptation today, resist it and let Jesus' victory be yours.*
- *If the enemy is trying to pull you down and discourage you, let Jesus' strength lift you up and cause you to stand firm.*
- *If you are facing fear or worry, let Jesus' peace be your confidence, your hope, and your security.*

The Kingdom of God is a kingdom of limitless power, ceaseless joy, and unending peace. It is a kingdom of righteousness, a kingdom of love, and a kingdom of right relationships. A friend of mine was once faced with a difficult decision that involved someone else. He thought about what would be best for him, and then he thought about what would be best for the other person. Finally, he thought about what would be best for the Kingdom. He knew he had made the right decision when he decided to do what was best for the Kingdom.

As you go through this day make every decision based upon what is best for the Kingdom, because what is best for the Kingdom is also what is best for you.

Today Is Your Best Day

Because You Serve the Lord (Part 1)

So, my dear brothers and sisters, be strong and steady,
always enthusiastic about the Lord's work,
for you know that nothing you do for the Lord is ever useless.
1 CORINTHIANS 15:58 NLT

God has given you the grace to know Him, the strength to obey Him, and the opportunity to serve Him in all you do today. There are certain things that are important for your heart to affirm as you continue your daily walk with Jesus. Here are three areas that are vital to your faith, your obedience, and your personal growth.

1. *You have an enemy that you must resist.* Satan does not like the fact that you have committed your life to Jesus Christ and that you are serving Him. He will oppose you, accuse you, and lie to you. He will try to tear you down and pull you down. He will use all his wiles to move your

eyes away from Jesus, or have your feet wander off the path that God has called you to follow. This is not a battle for you to win, but a battle that Jesus has already won. Stand fast in the victory that you have in Jesus Christ, and resist everything that is against God's will for you today.

2. *You have a call that is certain.* As you continue to walk in obedience to God and follow His heart today, you can affirm that you are doing what you're doing because God has called you to the place you're in. It's not your idea that placed you where you are, but God's. You are in God's place, in God's time. He hasn't made a mistake. You are where you are and doing what you are doing because it is part of God's plan and purpose for your life. You may be in a busy place or a quiet place, but the important thing is that it is God's place for you.

3. *You have a God who will not fail.* God has called you to trust in Him, to live in Him, and to follow Him. He hasn't called you to trust in your efforts but to trust in His grace; He hasn't called you to look to your resources, but to receive

His supply; He hasn't called you to struggle and strive, but to abide in His rest; He hasn't called you to lean upon your own understanding, but to depend upon His wisdom; He hasn't called you to be clever or talented, but to believe in His favor and blessing upon your life.

Everything that comes from God will succeed in fulfilling His perfect plan for your life. All that Jesus does in you and through you will make this your best day.

Today Is Your Best Day

Because You Serve the Lord
(Part 2)

Serve the LORD with gladness:
come before his presence with singing.
PSALM 100:2 KJV

Y
ou have so much to rejoice in today, so much to be glad for, so much to give praise for, and so much for your faith to celebrate. Today you have the awesome opportunity to serve the Lord. Think of it: The God who is majestic, all-powerful, altogether lovely, and altogether worthy wants to use you to reach out and touch others for His glory.

From His high and holy place He works through the lowly place of your heart to touch the hearts of those who are in need of a revelation of His love. Isaiah 57:15 (NLT) declares, "The high and lofty one who inhabits eternity, the Holy One, says this: 'I live in that high and holy place with those whose spirits are contrite and humble. I refresh the humble and give new courage to those with repentant hearts.' "

As God's servant you are in His hands as He conforms and transforms you into His image. In His hands, your life is the voice that speaks His words to those who need to know the truth; the hand that extends His love and mercies to those who are hurting; the example that demonstrates His kingdom to those who need to know the way. Today you have been given the awesome privilege of being used by Him and living for Him as you serve Him in your God-given place.

Today you are the bond servant of the righteous Master, the ambassador of the great King, and the messenger of the eternal Word. As His servant, you live for His approval, look for His smile, and labor for His glory. Your eyes are fixed upon His face, your heart is fixed upon His will, your ears are fixed upon His voice, and your life is fixed upon His pleasure. Your deepest motivation is not duty or obligation, but love. All that you do, you do for love's sake. Your "Yes" to His will is an obedience of love, your work is a labor of love, your praise is an offering of love, your giving is an extension of love, and your worship is an expression of love that comes from the deepest part of who you are.

Today Is Your Best Day

Because of Truth

*"However, when He, the Spirit of truth, has come, He will
guide you into all truth; for He will not speak on His
own authority, but whatever He hears He will speak;
and He will tell you things to come."*

JOHN 16:13 NKJV

As God's child there is nothing in the Truth of God
to depress you, defeat you, discourage you, or deflate
you. The Truth will build you up, lift you up, and
keep you up. The Truth has come to deliver you, free you, heal
you, restore you, refresh you, revive you, and renew you. Truth
brings you the light of God, the wisdom of God, the ways of
God, the plan of God, and the heart of God.

Truth is the belt that is tied around your spiritual armor to
keep it in place; it is the revelation of true goodness that draws
your heart to the Father's love; it is the burning lamp that
guides your feet on your pilgrim's journey; it is the plumb line
of righteousness that directs your obedience; it is the foundation of your faith and the road map that leads you through the

gates of salvation; it is the light in your spirit that brings you into worship and wonder; it is the mirror that your soul gazes into as you are beautified in His holiness; it is the protective servant that keeps you and prepares you to be Jesus' bride.

Truth is the light of God that overcomes the darkness of every lie that seeks to rob you of your peace, steal your joy, and quench your faith.

- *When the lie says, "God is not interested in you," the Truth says, "Cast all your cares upon Me, for I care for you."*
- *When the lie says, "God is against you," the Truth says, "Because God is for you, no one can be against you."*
- *When the lie says, "How could God love someone like you?" the Truth says, "God loves you with an everlasting love."*

Today is your best day as you know the Truth, receive the Truth, believe the Truth, obey the Truth, love the Truth, and embrace the Truth. Today, the Truth will set you free.

Today Is Your Best Day

Because of Humility (Part 1)

Likewise, ye younger, submit yourselves unto the elder. Yea, all of you be subject one to another, and be clothed with humility: for God resisteth the proud, and giveth grace to the humble.

1 PETER 5:5 KJV

Jesus, in His humility, left His exalted place in heaven and came to a lowly place on earth. In His humility He took on our humanity. As a man, He didn't seek out a place above men, nor did He seek out a place that was equal to men. Instead, He took the place below others and became the servant of all. In humility, He listened only to His Father and did only what His Father directed Him to do. He had no independent agenda.

Jesus' humility led Him to the lowest place of all—His suffering and the shedding of His blood upon the cross. Through Jesus' obedience of humility God raised Him up, exalted Him to the highest place, seated Him at His right hand, and gave Him a name that is above all names.

Today, as your heart seeks the lowly place, humility will move you toward everything that is good and away from everything that is evil. Humility is the pathway of every servant's journey. Humility is the road map that guides you to God's unconditional love, and it is the sign that points you to the vast treasure of His abundant grace.

Humility allows you to see your weakness and embrace God's strength; it allows you to see your insufficiency and embrace His adequacy; it allows you to see your emptiness and embrace His fullness; it allows you to see your poverty and embrace His riches; it allows you to see your sin and embrace His righteousness; it allows you to see your lack and embrace His supply.

Humility is the place of freedom where your spirit soars, where your love is perfected, and where God's richest blessings abound. Rivers never run from the valley to the mountaintop, but they always seek the lowest place, the place of least resistance. Today, as your heart is yielded to the Lord in humility, the river of the Holy Spirit will flood in and fill you to overflowing with peace, and flow out through you to bless the lives of others.

Today Is Your Best Day

Because of Humility (Part 2)

Therefore humble yourselves under the mighty hand of God,
that He may exalt you in due time.
1 PETER 5:6 NKJV

In his book *Humility*, Andrew Murray says, "Man's chief care, his highest virtue, and his only happiness, now and throughout eternity, is to present himself as an empty vessel in which God can dwell and manifest His power and goodness."

Two Christian men were having a conversation about their personal growth in the Lord. The first man stated, "I love being nothing. . . ."

Before the first man could finish his sentence the second man interrupted and said, "What do you mean by that? I don't understand why you would love being nothing."

"Well," replied the first man, "I love being nothing so that God can be my all in all."

Today is your best day because God wants you to live each moment totally and completely dependent upon Him. The response of humility in your heart affirms that Jesus is all you need, that He is more than sufficient, that He is altogether faithful, and that He will never fail you in any way through every circumstance of life.

Humility is not measured by what you do or don't do. It is not measured by what you say or how you look. Humility is measured by the attitude and disposition of your heart. It is measured by your surrender, your obedience, your faith, and your complete dependency upon God.

There are no limits to what God can do through the person who is free from pride and who, in humility, looks to God alone, trusts in God alone, receives from God alone, and responds to God alone.

Today, let your heart say, "Lord, I love being nothing, so that You can be my all in all."

Today Is Your Best Day

Because God Is Your All

Now when all things are made subject to Him, then the Son Himself will also be subject to Him who put all things under Him, that God may be all in all.

1 CORINTHIANS 15:28 NKJV

God fills all, sustains all, and has a purpose for all He has created. Here are some of the ways that He will bless your life as you trust and obey Him today.

- God is your shield and He will protect you (Psalm 18:30).
- God listens to all you say in prayer (Psalm 20:5).
- God will fulfill all that He has purposed for your life (Psalm 20:4).
- God will lead you with unfailing love (Psalm 25:10).
- God forgives all your sins (Psalm 25:18).
- God will delight you with His presence (Psalm 27:4).

- God will do everything that is right (Psalm 33:4).
- God will leave you in awe (Psalm 33:8).
- God will never give you unwise counsel (Psalm 73:24).
- God knows you completely and understands you perfectly (Psalm 33:15).
- God is, in His nature and His ways, always worthy of your praise (Psalm 34:1).
- God will free you from all your fears (Psalm 34:4).
- God will save you out of all your troubles (Psalm 34:17).
- God is someone you can rejoice in, be glad in, and celebrate today (Psalm 40:16).
- God is the King over all there is and all that concerns you (Psalm 47:2).
- God can be trusted at all times (Psalm 62:8).
- God is abundantly pouring out His mercy over you (Psalm 86:15).
- God is a great God to you (Psalm 95:3).
- God heals all your diseases (Psalm 103:3).
- God rules over all matters of your life (Psalm 103:19).
- God does wondrous things (Psalm 105:2).
- God does great things (Psalm111:2).

- God has done everything for you and will be everything to you (Psalm 116:12).
- God knows all your ways (Psalm 119:168).
- God will preserve you from all evil (Psalm 121:7).
- God's promises to you are backed by the honor of His name (Psalm 138:2).
- God saw you before you were born and has laid out a plan for your life (Psalm 139:16).
- God is good to you (Psalm 145:9).
- God lifts you up and upholds you (Psalm 145:14).
- God is near to you and is gracious to you (Psalm 145:17–18).
- God protects you (Psalm 145:20).

God is your all in all today.

I will tell everyone about your righteousness. All day long I will proclaim your saving power, for I am overwhelmed by how much you have done for me.
PSALM 71:15 NLT

Today Is Your Best Day

Because of God's Plan

"For I know the plans I have for you," declares the LORD,
"plans to prosper you and not to harm you, plans to give
you hope and a future."
JEREMIAH 29:11 NIV

G od has a plan for your life. He brought you into this world to fulfill that plan. It is the best plan that anyone could ever make. It is a plan that will bring Him the greatest glory and make you into all He desires you to be. Today is your best day because God is working out that plan.

God's plan may not take you in the direction you were expecting, it may not fit into your natural way of reasoning, and it may even seem to contradict what God has promised you. When Joseph was in his youth he saw his brothers bowing down to him, but Joseph never imagined that God would fulfill that dream by allowing him to be sold into slavery by those same brothers. Abraham had a promise from God that his son, Isaac, would be heir to God's covenant promise, but Abraham never thought that God would test his faith by asking him to offer

Isaac on an altar. Joseph and Mary had no plans of traveling to Bethlehem in the late stages of Mary's pregnancy, but a Roman census forced them to travel to the very place where the prophet declared Jesus would be born. Peter heard Jesus' promise to make him a fisher of men, but Peter, a devout Jew, had no idea that God would use him to bring the Gospel to the Gentiles.

As you follow God's plan for your life, you do so by faith. It is important to remember that He is the Guide and you are the follower. He is not going to bring you into His planning room as a consultant to help Him decide what is best for your life. God has not called you to question Him, but to trust Him and to take the next step of obedience according to His will. God has said, "I will bring the blind by a way they did not know; I will lead them in paths they have not known. I will make darkness light before them, and crooked places straight. These things I will do for them, and not forsake them" (Isaiah 42:16 NKJV).

If your life was like a painting, the strokes that are being added to the canvas today may not make much sense when viewed alone. However, God doesn't waste any strokes when He uses His divine brush, for He sees the final picture and knows exactly how each stroke will fit into the painting's finished image. You may think the color being used today is too gray and needs more brilliance, but the time will come when you will see that the painting would not be complete, and the meaning of the painting would be weakened, if the gray strokes were not included in the exact places they appear.

Today Is Your Best Day

Because of God's Wisdom

*O LORD, how manifold are thy works! in wisdom hast thou
made them all: the earth is full of thy riches.*

PSALM 104:24 KJV

God is wise. Everything He does for you is done in wisdom. Every decision He makes on your behalf is done in wisdom. God has perfect wisdom, which means that it is impossible for Him to make a mistake and that He never needs to redo or undo something He has done. God's wisdom means that He never takes a chance or makes a guess. God's wisdom is complete. He never gains wisdom or grows in wisdom, because He has all wisdom.

God's wisdom also means that He is skilled and that He is an expert in all He does. He is not a rookie who doesn't have enough experience, or an apprentice who is lacking in skills when it comes to managing your life.

I once went to get a medical test at a hospital. I was sent to an X-ray room where the test was going to be conducted. When I arrived in the room I was met by two nurses. One nurse introduced me to the other nurse and told me she was a new trainee and would be assisting in the procedure. The first thing that the trainee was asked to do was to put an IV into a vein in the top of my hand.

The trainee was very nice and pleasant, but because she didn't have a lot of experience she was very nervous. I hoped my smile would reassure her. She tried her best to successfully get the IV into my vein, but could not do it. At that point the skilled nurse stepped in and took over the rest of the procedure. She was able to hook up the IV with great ease and confidence.

> *God's hands are more skilled than a great surgeon;*
> *They are more tender than a caring nurse;*
> *They are more precise than a fine diamond cutter;*
> *They are more creative than the finest artist or designer.*

God's wisdom also means that He works in very practical ways in your life. God is your wise mentor, your practical helper, and your patient instructor. If your life was like a house, it would be built by a master builder; if your life was like a business, it would be run under the guidance of perfect management; if your life was like a tapestry, not a stitch would be misplaced or forgotten.

Today is your best day because God's wisdom is your portion, and He is skillfully working things out according to the counsel of His own will.

Today Is Your Best Day

Because of God's Knowledge

Then shalt thou understand the fear of the LORD, and find the knowledge of God. For the LORD giveth wisdom: out of his mouth cometh knowledge and understanding.
PROVERBS 2:5–6 KJV

God's knowledge means that God knows. What does God know? God knows everything about all things. God knows all about you. He knows you inside and out, and from top to bottom. He knows when you get up and when you lie down. He knows your actions, your thoughts, and your motivations. He knows everything there is to know about you. He even knows every hair on your head.

God knows all about your past, He knows all about your present, and He knows all about your future.

God's knowledge means that God foresees. Because God foresees, He is your perfect provider. God can make provision for your needs today because His knowledge allows Him to see your need before it happens. He saw yesterday the need that you have discovered today. No need that you face today has taken God by surprise or caught Him off guard. He doesn't wait for you to have a need before He comes up with a plan to solve it. His solution was made long before you discovered you had a need.

Many years ago I was doing missionary work in Mexico. One day my coworkers and I decided to take a fact-finding trip to a city that was located many hours away. In order to get to the city we would need to drive through a large mountain range. Our main purpose in taking the trip was to find someone who could provide us with information about the missionary work being done in the city and the surrounding area.

As we were winding our way through the mountains, we heard a loud explosion. It didn't take us long to realize that our rear tire had blown out. We guided our truck as close to the side of the road as we could and got out. The tire was destroyed and could not be patched. To make matters worse, we had no spare. What to do? We all gathered at the back of the truck and prayed, asking God to meet our need and take care of the situation.

We had no sooner said "Amen" than a vehicle came around the curve. The driver slowed down and pulled in behind us. Out stepped a tall American who introduced himself and asked if he could be of any help. When he heard our story he immediately replied, "I have an extra tire in the back of my truck that I believe is the same size as yours." The tire was the exact fit. We also discovered that the man was a missionary who was returning from a six-week visit to the States and that he lived in the city we were going to visit. He turned out to be the perfect contact for us.

The Lord knows all about you today and He knows what is best. You can be certain that His knowledge will cover you from the start of the day until its end.

Today Is Your Best Day

Because of God's Presence

And He said, "My Presence will go with you, and I will give you rest." Then he said to Him, "If Your Presence does not go with us, do not bring us up from here."
EXODUS 33:14–15 NKJV

There is something better than having what is best in your day, and that is having the One who is the best. God is the best Person you could ever know, the best Friend you could ever trust, and the best Companion you can ever have. God's presence is sweet, enjoyable, and delightful.

God gives you what is best because He is the best. God gives the best kind of peace. Jesus said that He would give you His peace, not the peace that the world gives. The world's peace is fragile, uncertain, and easily toppled. God's peace can withstand any storm and difficulty of life. His peace brings the glorious assurance that all is well because you are His and He is yours.

God gives the best kind of joy. Jesus said He wanted our joy to be full. The world can only give momentary happiness based upon momentary pleasures, but God gives fullness of joy, a joy that runs deeper than any circumstance of life.

God gives the best kind of love. His love is unconditional. God never says, "Give me a reason to love you." God loves you with a perfect love. He doesn't need a reason to love you because He *is* love, and He loves you with an everlasting love. Today, His heart of love calls out for you to love Him with all of your heart.

There is a reason why God calls out for you to love Him with all your heart. God loves you with a perfect love. His perfect love can only desire what is the highest, the greatest, and the absolute best for your life. If He would desire anything else for you, He would be saying that He would rather have you know and experience what is second best.

God commands you to love Him because He is the highest choice and the greatest good that you could ever choose. God could never say to you, "Love people more than Me; love doing good more than Me; love life more than Me; love ministry more than Me." All of these things, as good as they are in themselves, can be enemies of the best when they are in the wrong place in our lives.

Peace is yours today, joy is yours, love is yours, because God's presence is yours, and His presence means the very best.

Today Is Your Best Day

Because of Love

God has poured out his love to fill our hearts. God gave us his love through the Holy Spirit, whom God has given to us.
ROMANS 5:5 ICB

"If you believe in me, come and drink! For the Scriptures declare that rivers of living water will flow out from within."
JOHN 7:38 NLT

God is love and His love is the best kind of love you can have in your heart. The beautiful thing about God's love is that it is a giving love—a love that flows in abundance with kindness, generosity, and goodness. It is a love that embraces and does not push away. It is a love that restores, mends, and heals.

It is a love of compassion, good will, and tender care.

The love that God has poured into you is also the love that He wants to pour out through you. Today is your best day because you have the awesome privilege and opportunity to give His love away to other people. The love that you are able to give to others is not something that you make up or pretend to have. You are not the source of the love you can give away; God is the source. God's love is not received into your life through study or good works. His love is yours because the Holy Spirit has come to live in your heart.

The Holy Spirit has come to live in you like a river, not like a lake. A river flows and moves freely. A lake sits and goes nowhere. A river reaches out to new places and nourishes new ground. A lake is self-contained and can become stagnant. The love of God in you first comes to bless and enrich your life, but its course is to flow out from within you to touch and enrich other hearts.

Be sensitive to the Holy Spirit's leading of love in your life today. Count upon His love, lean upon His love, and draw upon His love to be the source of God's love through you. It may be expressed through a prayer you offer, through a word you speak, through an embrace you extend, through a kindness you perform, or even through a smile you give.

Today Is Your Best Day

Because of God's Timing

My times are in Your hand.
PSALM 31:15 NKJV

When I was a child, two of my favorite books were about trains. One was called *Little Toot* and the other was *The Little Engine That Could*. It seems like I've always had a special interest in trains. I enjoyed watching electric trains in store windows during Christmastime, and begged my parents for an electric train set of my own. As a boy I made several train trips on the Santa Fe lines from the West Coast to the East and loved every minute of it.

Trains can teach us some important lessons about life. Trains leave from stations, run on schedules, wait on other trains while en route, have stop and go signals to obey, and carry important cargo to various destinations. Trains also need upkeep and maintenance.

Like a train, your life has a starting point and a final destination. It runs on a divinely appointed schedule and makes important stops along the way. People move in and out of your life like passengers would on a train, and there are stop-lights and go lights along the way. You have a powerful engine, the Holy Spirit, who moves you along on the tracks of faith and obedience, and like the train, you are well kept and maintained by God's Word.

God, like a skilled engineer and the owner of the line, is the One who makes your schedule and keeps everything running on His timetable. He knows when you need to leave a station in life and when you need to arrive at the next one. Along the way He brings people in and out of your life so that you can minister to them and they can minister to you. God is also in your stops and starts, and although your journey may sometimes seem slow, God knows exactly where you are and what He is doing.

Today is your best day because you are exactly where God wants you to be in this phase of your journey. It may be that you are waiting for Him to fulfill His promise to you, or you are anxious to move into something new, but God wants you to wait on Him until He is ready to fulfill what He has promised. Waiting times are not wasted times with God. While you are waiting, it does not mean that God is not working. There may be some dangers up ahead or some obstacles on the tracks that first need to be removed before God moves you on in His will. Today if you are waiting at a station or moving on, full speed ahead, the important thing to remember is that the best place to be is exactly where God has you at this moment.

Today Is Your Best Day

Because of the Blood of Jesus

Knowing that you were not redeemed with corruptible things,
like silver or gold, from your aimless conduct received by tradi-
tion from your fathers, but with the precious blood of Christ,
as of a lamb without blemish and without spot.

1 PETER 1:18–19 NKJV

How greatly blessed, honored, and favored you are today because of the blood of Jesus Christ. Without His precious blood your day would be covered in darkness, hopelessness, and despair; instead, your day is flooded with light, filled with hope, and enriched with every spiritual blessing. The blood of Jesus has taken you from the dungeons of slavery and brought you into the highway of holiness; it has delivered you from the cruelty of a harsh taskmaster and brought you into the tender care of a loving Father; it has saved you from a life that was a descending stairway of bondage, into an ascending life of freedom that lifts you from glory to glory.

The blood of Jesus cleanses you from the stain of sin, looses you from the chains of sin, frees you from the power of sin, saves you from the judgment of sin, and heals you from the pain of sin. The blood of Jesus restores and reconciles you to God. The blood of Jesus not only makes it possible for you to be forgiven, but it also makes it possible for you to be fully cleansed.

Once, a little boy was dressed in his best clothes for Sunday morning church. The boy's mother told him not to go outside and play, but to wait in the house until everyone was ready to go to church. The boy sat on a chair for a while but soon became restless. He got up from the chair and looked out the window. He spotted the family dog chasing a rabbit and decided he would get in on the fun.

The boy came back into the house moments before the family was ready to leave. To her dismay, the mother discovered that the boy was covered with mud. Teary-eyed, the boy repentantly told his mother what had happened and that he was sorry he disobeyed her. The mother did forgive the boy, but she didn't stop there. The mother saw to it that the boy's dirty clothes were changed, and that he was washed clean with another bath, before they left for church.

Why is today your best day? It is your best day because the blood of Jesus has not lost its power (and it will *never* lose its power) to make it possible for you to begin this day forgiven, to be clothed in garments of righteousness, and to face the day with clean hands and a pure heart.

Today Is Your Best Day

Because of Redemption

Neither by the blood of goats and calves, but by his [Jesus'] own blood he entered in once into the holy place, having obtained eternal redemption for us.

HEBREWS 9:12 KJV

Jesus Christ is your Redeemer and His shed blood has secured your redemption. The Bible tells us that we were all prisoners who were held captive, without the hope of freedom, unless a ransom price was paid to free us. The blood of Jesus Christ is the ransom price that was paid to set us free from the captivity of Satan and the enslavement of sin. If a wealthy man paid all that he had to free his son from a person who was holding him captive, that ransom amount would give us some idea of what the life of that son was worth to his father. God paid a much higher price to redeem you and bring you back to Him.

I have enjoyed going to auctions throughout the years. One of the things that I find interesting about auctions is how much collectors and dealers are willing to pay for an item that comes up for bid. They seem to know what things are worth and are not afraid to bid on items they know are valuable. One lesson you can learn from an auction is that an item is only worth what someone is willing to pay.

The price to redeem you cost God everything. How much were you worth to God? What was your true value? You need only look to the blood of Jesus Christ to understand. You were worth, to God, the death of His Son. God paid more to redeem you than the total wealth there is upon the earth.

When the Bible says that you have been redeemed, it means that you have been absolutely freed, fully released, and totally delivered from all that had you bound in the past. Redemption also means that you have been redeemed from the guilt and condemnation that sin had over you. Today is your best day because you are a free man or woman who never needs to be enslaved again.

Today is your best day because God was willing to pay the price of the death of His Son to redeem you as His own. God has redeemed you, not to set you aside, ignore you, or let you get dusty on a shelf. He has redeemed you because He loves you, cares about you, treasures you, and has a plan and purpose for your life.

Today Is Your Best Day

Because Jesus Is 100 Percent

This High Priest of ours understands our weaknesses, for he faced all of the same temptations we do, yet he did not sin.

Hebrews 4:15 NLT

Baseball and basketball are very popular sports. Most teams draw large crowds and have a wide television and radio audience. One thing that is amazing about these sports is that their fans can get excited over athletes who fail far more often than they succeed. In baseball, if a batter can get a hit more than 40 percent of the time, he would be considered a phenomenon. In basketball, if a player made more baskets than he missed during his career, he would be considered the greatest offensive player of all time.

No matter where we look in life, people never perform to perfection. There are shortcomings, disappointments, and failures everywhere we turn. Anything human, or made by humans, eventually breaks down or doesn't perform according to our expectations.

The other day I was driving with my wife along a winding

road that worked its way through some tree-lined bluffs. As we made our way down the picturesque country road, my wife remembered that she needed to call a friend and give her an important message. She got her cell phone out of her purse, flipped open the lid, and waited for a signal. No signal appeared and the phone call couldn't be made. As she closed the lid on the cell phone and returned it to her purse she turned to me and said, "Nothing in life can be depended upon 100 percent, except Jesus."

Even though everything around you is flawed and imperfect, today is your best day because you have Jesus. Jesus is 100 percent perfect in all His ways, in all He is, and in all He does. Think of it—the perfect Son of God left heaven, came to earth as a man, and lived among us. In His thirty-three-plus years on earth He never sinned. Never! His Father sent Him here as the spotless Lamb of God who would offer Himself upon the cross as a sacrifice for your sins. Jesus fully obeyed His Father, and through His perfect obedience He glorified the Father. If Jesus would have sinned, even once, He could not have died for your sins on the cross. You would be lost and without hope today.

In His nature and character, Jesus is without fault or flaw. He is completely faithful. He cannot fail you, and He will not fail you. Every promise He has made is true; there is not one lie or exaggeration in anything that He has ever said. Today, Jesus is your 100 percent Savior.

Jesus did not let you down when He lived on earth; He did not let you down when He died on the cross; He did not let you down when He rose from the dead; He did not let you down when He was seated at the right hand of the Father. Jesus will not let you down today.

Today Is Your Best Day

Because of Joy

And the ransomed of the Lord shall return, and come to Zion
with songs and everlasting joy upon their heads: they shall obtain
joy and gladness, and sorrow and sighing shall flee away.
ISAIAH 35:10 KJV

J oy is one of the great benefits and blessings of the Kingdom
of God within your life. Joy is the melody of heaven that
is placed in your heart; joy is the Holy Spirit's symphony
that is played within your spirit; joy is the theme song of every
person who trusts in the Lord and knows His love.

Joy is the highest level of delight that a person can experience. Human happiness is dependent upon the experiences
and circumstances of life, while joy is dependent upon God
alone. God, not your personality type, is the source of your
joy. Today, joy flows from His heart to yours like a fountain
that will never run dry.

It is easy to think that joy can come from other things apart
from God. We can anticipate the joys that a new house will
bring us, or the delight that a car will be to us once we have it,

but there is no lasting satisfaction in any material thing that we possess. This does not mean that these things cannot be a blessing to us when God provides them, but they can never replace the true joys that come to us from God alone.

The joy that comes from God gives you strength. A joyless person is someone whose strength is depleted. Joy invigorates, motivates, and inspires. Joy is like energy that flows through you to lighten your load, renew your zeal, and quicken your steps of faith. Joy is the strength in your legs that helps you stand firm and steady in times of trial; the power in your arms that enables you to hold on to God's exceeding great and precious promises; the rejoicing in your voice that speaks forth the victory of the Lord over every area of your life.

God not only wants you to have His joy reigning in your heart today, but He wants your joy to become great joy, and He wants great joy to become the fullness of joy. God wants you to be immersed in the delights of His joy today, soaking you through and through, so that every fiber of your being is filled with praises, rejoicing, and celebration of His goodness.

We move into the highest levels of joy when we abide in the love of the Father, and through Him, reach out to love others. Today is your best day as you allow the Father to fill you with His love, love others through you, and as you walk in the fullness of His joy.

Today Is Your Best Day

Because of Peace

Now the Lord of peace himself give you peace always by all means. The Lord be with you all.

2 THESSALONIANS 3:16 KJV

Peace is such a precious gift from the Lord. Peace has been defined in many ways—calm in the midst of a storm, quiet in the midst of turmoil, tranquility in the midst of uncertainty. The presence of peace is the absence of confusion and strife. Peace can also be defined as the deep and unshakable conviction that all is well with your soul. Peace comes when your heart is confident that God is in control, not only of the universe, but of your life, as well. Peace also comes by knowing that God is for you and by being in harmony with God as you live from day to day.

Peace is also the *shalom* of God. One of God's names is Jehovah-Shalom. It means that God not only gives peace, but He *is* peace. Shalom is a word that embraces God's favor, blessing, prosperity, health, welfare, rest, wholeness, and friendship.

There was a time when my family and I went to Puerto Rico to become part of a missionary team on the island. Before we left the United States, we turned over our possessions to the missionary group that was sending us. It was something we were happy to do, thinking we would be a part of the mission for a long time. The way things turned out, we only stayed with the mission for a year.

Our return flight to the States took us to Los Angeles International Airport. When my wife, our two children, and I arrived at LAX, we got our luggage and walked outside to wait for our ride. As we waited, I looked down at our five pieces of luggage that stood at my feet. In those five suitcases were all the possessions we owned. I had a few dollars in my wallet, no money in the bank, and no idea what I would be doing next.

It was in that moment that a deep sense of God's peace came flooding over me.

I had never known peace at that depth before. I was overwhelmed and overjoyed. Quietly, in that moment, I heard God's still small voice speak these words to my heart: "My peace does not depend upon what you have or don't have. No matter how many possessions you may acquire from this time on, none of them can add one ounce of peace to your life." As I stood there soaking in what God was saying, I also heard Him say, "Any possession you may lose from this point on cannot take one ounce of My peace away from you."

Today is your best day because the God of peace and the peace of God is your portion—a peace that no circumstance, thing, or person can either increase or diminish.

Today Is Your Best Day

Because of Grace (Part 1)

*But God, who is rich in mercy, because of His great love with
which He loved us, even when we were dead in trespasses, made
us alive together with Christ (by grace you have been saved). . .
that in the ages to come He might show the exceeding riches
of His grace in His kindness toward us in Christ Jesus.
For by grace you have been saved through faith,
and that not of yourselves; it is the gift of God.*
EPHESIANS 2:4–5, 7–8 NKJV

Grace makes it possible for today to be your best day.
Grace demands nothing and gives everything God
desires you to have. Through grace, God has pulled
out all the stops, and poured His abundant favor upon you
in Jesus Christ. Grace points you to Jesus and says, "All that
is His is freely yours. All mercy, all blessings, all strength, all
righteousness, all kindness is yours today in Jesus Christ."

When someone has a job, he expects to get paid because he
has earned his wages. Pay is given to him based strictly upon
his performance. The longer a person stays on a job the more

he expects to get paid. If he remains a good and loyal employee, he will usually get promoted and take on more benefits. This merit of pay and benefits has nothing to do with grace, but rather with works.

God does not want you to try to earn His favor. He's not looking at the number of years you have been a Christian to decide how much He should bless you. You are not blessed today based upon your tenure in Christ.

Grace means that you do not need to earn something that you have already been given. Even when you need more grace, God supplies it freely. How did you receive grace in the first place? God did not extend His grace to you because you were a nice sinner, a sincere sinner, or a disciplined sinner. He extended His grace to you while you were a sinner, no matter what kind of sinner you were. He did not extend His grace to you because you were religious or full of good works. God's grace came to you through the cross. He extended His grace to you, not based upon what you did for Him, but based upon what His Son did for you.

God extends grace to you today, as His child, as He did when you were a sinner. Nothing that you have done as a believer in Christ has earned you more grace. Bible reading, prayer, giving, and Christian service don't mean that you have earned the right to have more grace poured out upon you. If it did, grace would not be grace. Whenever the word "grace" appears in the scriptures, there is another word that often appears nearby. That word is *given*. You will never find the word *deserved* associated with grace.

Every joy that fills your heart and every delight that satisfies your soul are yours today because of the benefits of grace. God has showered you with these favors without any expectation of return. Grace does not hang something over your head and say, "You owe Me and I expect you to pay Me back." Grace is the absolute free expression of God's loving heart. The motivation of grace is to bountifully bless you.

Today Is Your Best Day

Because of Grace
(Part 2)

*Who hath saved us, and called us with an holy calling,
not according to our works, but according to his own
purpose and grace, which was given us in
Christ Jesus before the world began.*

2 TIMOTHY 1:9 KJV

There are so many benefits of grace that are yours
today.

- *Salvation:* You are saved by grace. The
  forgiveness of your sins, your justification before
  God, your redemption from the slavery of sin,
  your deliverance from evil, and your future
  home in heaven are yours today because of
  grace.

- *Sufficiency:* Grace enables you to do all God calls
  you to do today. Success is not based upon what

you can accomplish, but upon what He will do through you. Grace is not about your strength, but about His power working in you, even in the time of your greatest weakness.

- *Edification:* Grace builds you up, lifts you up, and keeps you standing. Grace is heard in the sound of God's voice speaking over and over into your ear, "I am for you today. I am with you today. I am the source of everything good, everything lovely, everything holy, and everything mighty."

- *Hope:* Grace assures you of a glorious future and an overwhelming inheritance that is yours in Jesus Christ. Grace leads you on, cheers you on, and moves you on into all that is in God's heart for you.

- *Victory:* Grace brings to you all that is yours in Christ. You are victorious today because Jesus is the triumphant One. You are more than a conqueror because He has conquered all. You are above all things because all things are under His feet. You reign in life because He reigns—King of kings and Lord of lords.

- *Abundance:* Where sin once abounded, grace abounds even more. Where darkness ruled, grace overruled. Where death held you in cruel bondage, grace brought you into a glorious new freedom. Grace is never poured out to you like raindrops, but like a cascading waterfall.

- *Purity:* Grace is the doorway into the beauty of God's holiness. Grace is never a license to sin, a freedom to sin, or a cloak for sin. Grace brings us into a life that is greater than what sin could ever offer us. Grace extends the hand that lifts us out of the miry clay, throws the rope that pulls us from the deepest pit, and lights the flame that brings us out of the darkest cave.

- *Gifting:* Gifts that come to you from God are grace gifts. His grace gifts to you will be different than the grace gifts He gives to others. Grace does not play favorites. The gifts that have been given to you from God are the perfect gifts that are needed for you to fulfill His will and His calling in your life.

Today Is Your Best Day

Because of Grace (Part 3)

*And God is able to make all grace abound toward you;
that ye, always having all sufficiency in all things,
may abound to every good work.*
2 Corinthians 9:8 kjv

Grace abounds to you today with so many favors, blessings, and joys.

- Without His grace we were songbirds without a song; by His grace we have been given a new song to sing and a melody of praise for our hearts to rejoice in.

- Without His grace we were trees bearing bitter fruit; by His grace we bear sweet fruit, lush fruit, and fruit that remains.

- Without His grace our heads hung low and turned away from the light of His love; by His grace our heads have been lifted up and our hearts have been flooded with His glorious light.

- Without His grace we were defenseless against the attacks of the enemy; by His grace we stand against the enemy triumphantly—completely equipped with the full armor of God, the blood of Jesus, the power of the Holy Spirit, and the ministry of the heavenly host.

- Without His grace we lived in confusion, were lost, and had no clear direction; by His grace we have been found, and His wisdom guides our lives as He makes straight paths for our feet.

- Without His grace our words had no message, and we gave our opinion only to have it drowned out by the opinions of others; by His grace He has put His sure and certain words in our mouths. We can now speak the truth in love and know that the Word of God abides forever.

- Without His grace we were blind, stumbling about in the darkness, trying to find our purpose and make a way for ourselves in the world; by His grace our eyes have been opened, our purpose has been made known, our hearts are set on eternity, and we daily walk in the good things that He has prepared for us.

- Without His grace we were fearful, motivated by self-interests, and striving to succeed; by His grace we have entered into His rest, we walk in His peace, and we daily live for His glory.

- Without His grace we were without hope, without the assurance of heaven, and bound by the fear of death; by His grace we abound in hope, we rejoice in the certainty of the resurrection, and we glory in knowing that the very best is still ahead.

Today Is Your Best Day

Because of the Holy Spirit
(Part 1)

"Nevertheless I tell you the truth; It is expedient for you that I go away: for if I go not away, the Comforter will not come unto you; but if I depart, I will send him unto you."
JOHN 16:7 KJV

Today is your best day because Jesus sent the Holy Spirit. The Holy Spirit is our divine companion, our comforter, and the one who has come alongside us. How greatly blessed we are to have the Holy Spirit within our lives, abiding with us, speaking to us, and walking with us as we go through our day.

The Holy Spirit is truer than the truest friend. Every pleasing quality of a close and tender friend is found in the Holy Spirit. He knows everything about you, loves you without reservation or condition, cares about every need you face, and will never betray your trust. The Holy Spirit is completely dependable, fully available, and totally reliable.

Jesus sent the Holy Spirit, not to be with you partially so

you could have a little taste of His presence, but to be in your life in fullness. Jesus wants you to be submerged in, clothed with, and empowered by the Holy Spirit. The Bible tells us that the Holy Spirit has come to be with you, to be in you, to fill you, and to come upon you.

The Holy Spirit has been sent to take you deeper into the love of God. The ocean is a great expanse and its depths are beginning to be explored in new ways. Unaided, man can only descend a short distance into the ocean's depths. Modern technology and engineering have created machines that can carry man to depths never before thought possible. The Holy Spirit can take you into the depths of God's love that you've never seen, known, or understood before.

The Holy Spirit has also been sent to take you higher and allow your eyes to see more of the greatness and glory of God's majesty. Through the space program, man has been able to explore new heights, seeing things and doing things that were thought impossible a century ago. The Holy Spirit can cause your spirit to ascend into the heights of God's glory, to behold the beauty of the Lord, and to celebrate His majesty with a heart that is in awe of His splendor.

Today Is Your Best Day

Because of the Holy Spirit (Part 2)

*And now you also have heard the truth, the Good News that
God saves you. And when you believed in Christ, he
identified you as his own by giving you the Holy Spirit,
whom he promised long ago.*

EPHESIANS 1:13 NLT

The Holy Spirit is wonderful! He has feelings that
reach out to you in compassion and love; He has a
mind that thinks about you and plans good for you;
He has a will that chooses the highest and the best for you. His
purpose is to bring to pass all that God has planned for you, to
make real all that Jesus has done for you, and to reveal all that
the scriptures declare to you.

The Holy Spirit was involved in your life, long before you
put your trust in Jesus Christ. The Holy Spirit pursued you
when you walked according to your way; He wooed you to
the heart of God when your heart was fixed upon other things;
He called you to follow God's divine purpose when you were

seeking plans of your own; He brought you into the light of God's truth when you stumbled about in darkness; He drew you into the arms of Jesus when you were in need of love's lasting embrace.

The Holy Spirit points you to Jesus' life, Jesus' character, and to Jesus' works. The Holy Spirit opens Jesus' worthiness to your spirit; He opens Jesus' wisdom to your understanding; He opens Jesus' love to your heart. The Holy Spirit has come to keep you from defeat, discouragement, and despair. The Holy Spirit's voice brings hope, assurance, peace, and revelation. His encouragement is the greatest when your valleys are the deepest; His comfort is the sweetest when your burdens are the heaviest; His support is the strongest when your strength is the weakest; His love is the surest when your fears are the vastest.

Today is your best day because of the calling, the gifting, the enabling, and the empowering of the Holy Spirit upon your life.

Because of the Holy Spirit (Part 3)

And straightway coming up out of the water, he saw the heavens opened, and the Spirit like a dove descending upon him.
MARK 1:10 KJV

To help you understand the impact and importance of the ministry of the Holy Spirit in your life, the Bible uses various symbols to describe Him.

• *The Holy Spirit is likened to the wind.* He can come to you as a mighty wind, bringing God's awesome power as He did at the day of Pentecost. His power will give you great boldness and fully equip you for what God has prepared for you today. The Holy Spirit can also come to you as a gentle breeze, cooling you and delighting you with His sweet presence. Like the wind, the Holy Spirit is also the breath of God that quickens you and brings you spiritual life.

The Holy Spirit is the atmosphere of heaven that your spirit breathes.

- *The Holy Spirit is likened to a dove.* As a dove, The Holy Spirit can come upon you in a tender, gentle way as He did when He came upon Jesus after His baptism in the river Jordan. The Holy Spirit will also hover over your life as He hovered over the waters at the time of creation. This hovering is likened to a bird as she flutters over her young with her wings. Like the protective bird, the Holy Spirit guards your life and watches over the good work that God has begun in you.

- *The Holy Spirit is likened to a river.* He moves in your life in a flowing motion, directing you one way, and then another, according to God's will and purpose for your life. His life in you never becomes stagnant or stale. He is an abundant river within you. The headwaters begin at the throne of God and flow out with mercy and grace. He flows deeply within you, and His sparkling clear waters brilliantly reflect the sunlight of Jesus' perfect love.

- *The Holy Spirit is likened to fire.* He is the flame that lights the candle of your spirit and causes you to look upon Jesus' beautiful face. He illuminates your way and opens your understanding, causing you to see things you've never seen before. His flame is also a purifying fire that burns away the empty things in your life, leaving only those things that have an eternal value—gold, silver, and precious stones (1 Corinthians 3:12–13).

- *The Holy Spirit is likened to oil.* The Holy Spirit is the One who is poured out upon you like a healing balm—to soothe, to calm, and to comfort. He is the One who renews your strength, revives your spirit, refills your cup, restores your strength, and refreshes your spirit. The Holy Spirit is being poured out upon you today.

Today Is Your Best Day

Because of God's Promises
(Part 1)

They are the people of Israel, chosen to be God's special children.
God revealed his glory to them. He made covenants with them
and gave his law to them. They have the privilege of worshiping
him and receiving his wonderful promises.

ROMANS 9:4 NLT

You have so much going for you today, because so much has been given to you by God. You have the fullness of His grace, the bounty of His mercies, the greatness of His power, the beauty of His presence, and the wonders of His love. You have been blessed with the fellowship of other believers, the revelation of the sacred scriptures, the daily intercession of Jesus Christ, the watchful ministry of heavenly angels, and you have been given the precious promises spoken from the heart of God.

God's promises are like golden apples given to you in baskets of silver, providing a treasure of priceless worth. They are like an oasis that you've found in the desert, bordered with lush, date-bearing palm trees, and surrounded by pools of pristine water. They are like a feast offered to you on the banqueting table of the King, loaded with fresh bread, the finest wine, food fixed to perfection, and desserts that are a delight to taste.

Any promise that is made to you is only as reliable as the character of the one who made it. People can promise many things that they are unable or unwilling to do. God is not like that. Every promise that He has made is sure and certain. God's promises are completely reliable because God is completely dependable. The God who created all there is stands behind all He has promised.

God's promises are true because God cannot lie. Truth is part of God's nature and character. God doesn't only *know* truth or *have* truth, He *is* Truth. God never wavers between "yes" and "no" when it comes to fulfilling His promises. In Jesus Christ, God has already said yes to every promise He has made.

God has given you His promises because He wants you to know what is in His heart for you today.

> *If you have tears today, there are promises of comfort;*
> *If you have heaviness, there are promises of joy;*
> *If you are in need of direction, there are promises of*
>   *guidance;*
> *If you need to make an important decision, there are*

promises of wisdom;
If you have doubts, there are promises of assurance;
If you are facing trials, there are promises of victory;
If you are in sin, there are promises of cleansing and
*   forgiveness;*
If you are in sickness, there are promises of healing;
If you are in conflict, there are promises of peace.

God's promises not only assure you that He will give you all that is best today, but that His best will also be a glorious part of your future.

Today Is Your Best Day

Because of God's Promises
(Part 2)

As we know Jesus better, his divine power gives us everything we need for living a godly life. He has called us to receive his own glory and goodness! And by that same mighty power, he has given us all of his rich and wonderful promises. . . . So make every effort to apply the benefits of these promises to your life. Then your faith will produce a life of moral excellence. A life of moral excellence leads to knowing God better.

2 PETER 1:3–5 NLT

Your position in Christ today means that you have a great heritage to claim, great benefits to enjoy, great promises to embrace, and great blessings to receive.

God doesn't want you to simply know *about* His promises or give them a casual nod, but He wants your faith to actively reach out and *take* them as your own.

I once knew someone who had just purchased the latest edition of a planning calendar. He was excited about its many features and felt that the planner would help him get better organized. A few days after he bought his planning calendar he made an appointment with me. When the day of the appointment came I showed up at the designated meeting place. I was on time, but the other person wasn't there. I waited a long time for him to arrive, but he never came. To my surprise, when I called him to find out why he wasn't at our meeting, he embarrassingly replied, "I'm so sorry. I completely forgot!"

When God makes a promise to you He never fails to keep His promise because He never forgets. God doesn't need a planning book to help Him remember what He has promised to you, or what He has planned for you. His promise book is the Word of God and He knows everything that is in it, down to the smallest detail.

Sometimes people make sincere promises to others, only to discover that they don't have the resources to make their promise good. A father may promise his son a specific toy for Christmas, only to discover that the toy has been sold out and will no longer be available. God never fails to keep a promise He has made to you because of limited resources or because what He has promised you in Christ is no longer available. God never fails to deliver on what He has said. Every promise that God has made will cause you to know Him better, enjoy Him more fully, and love Him more deeply. His promises are yours today.

Consider this promise that He has made to you from the thirteenth chapter of Hebrews:

Let your character or *moral disposition be free from love of money [including greed, avarice, lust, and craving for earthly possessions] and be satisfied with your present [circumstances and with what you have]; for He [God] Himself has said, I will not in any way fail you* nor *give you up* nor *leave you without support. [I will] not, [I will] not, [I will] not in any degree leave you helpless* nor *forsake* nor *let [you] down (relax My hold on you)! [Assuredly not!] So we take comfort* and *are encouraged* and *confidently* and *boldly say, The Lord is my Helper; I will not be seized with alarm [I will not fear or dread or be terrified]. What can man do to me?*

(HEBREWS 13:5–6 AMPLIFIED)

Today Is Your Best Day

Because of God's Character

"But let him who glories glory in this, that he understands and knows Me, that I am the LORD, exercising lovingkindness, judgment, and righteousness in the earth. For in these I delight."
JEREMIAH 9:24 NKJV

There is no one like God. He transcends all that He has made. He is more majestic than the great mountain peaks that rise above the ground; He is more lovely than the beautiful flowers that bloom along the countryside; He is more awesome than the sun as it sets in all its brilliance; He is more diverse than all the trees that fill the forests, that bear fruit in their season, and that shade the landscapes of every country path and village square.

God's character is the foundation that you build your life upon, the rock that your feet stand upon, and the strong tower that your faith leans upon. God is completely dependable, unshakable, unmovable, and totally reliable.

What does your faith in God's character mean to you today? It means that you know the sun still shines even though there are dark clouds overhead; that the anchor of your soul still holds even though the storm rages on; that your next step is certain even though a heavy fog covers your pathway; that comfort will be your portion even though you are facing a dark valley; that a strong hand is holding yours even though there is nothing to hang on to as you walk near the mountain's edge.

Today is in God's hands, and so are you. His hands are strong and they will uphold you; His hands are great and they will enfold you; His hands are gentle and they will embrace you; His hands are protective and they will cover you; His hands are powerful and they will defend you; His hands are compassionate and they will care for you.

Consider these truths from Psalm 46 as you trust in His character today:

> *God is our refuge and strength,*
> *always ready to help in times of trouble.*
> *So we will not fear, even if earthquakes come*
> *and the mountains crumble into the sea. . . .*
> *The LORD Almighty is here among us;*
> *the God of Israel is our fortress. . . .*
> *"Be silent, and know that I am God! . . .*
> *The LORD Almighty is here among us.*
> PSALM 46:1–2, 7, 10–11 NLT

Today is your best day because the One who holds you up will never let you down!

Today Is Your Best Day

Because of God's Leading
(Part 1)

For thou art my rock and my fortress;
therefore for thy name's sake lead me, and guide me.
PSALM 31:3 KJV

Today is your best day because God will lead you in His paths, guide your way, and direct your steps. Today, you will take steps you have never taken before, learn things you've never known before, and have opportunities you've never been given before. God has many methods of showing you His ways and leading you in His will. Some of these include the Holy Scriptures, the voice of the Holy Spirit, the wise counsel of godly people, His provisions, and His peace within your heart.

God will lead you into new discoveries of spiritual truth, into new places of ministry, into new relationships, into new discoveries of prayer, into new avenues of praise, into new adventures of faith, into new steps of obedience, or into new ways of practically expressing His love to others.

I once worked with a good friend in a growing business. One day, as we stepped out of the building to take a brief work break, I sensed God's still small voice prompting me to give my friend a dollar bill. At first I hesitated, thinking that it was too small of an amount to bother with, and that my friend might think it silly of me to give it to him. The prompting, however, continued to pull upon my heart. Finally, I opened my wallet, took out a dollar bill, and handed it to my friend. "Here," I said, "I'm not sure why I am giving you this, but I sense that the Lord wants you to have it."

We didn't talk about the matter after we returned to work, but my curiosity over the dollar bill remained with me for the rest of the day. The next morning, when I met my friend at work, he shared an interesting story with me. "Do you remember the dollar you gave me yesterday?" he asked. "Yes," I quickly replied. "Well," he continued, "I didn't think it was a very significant thing yesterday morning, but I changed my mind before the day was over. Late yesterday afternoon I had an appointment at the doctor's office. I thought I had taken enough cash with me to pay for the visit, but when I went to pay my bill I discovered I was a dollar short. I remembered the dollar bill you gave me, pulled it out of my pocket, and added it to the amount I had in my wallet."

That story turned out to be a great blessing to both of us, not because God had provided a huge sum of money for my friend, but because God showed both of us how much He loves us and cares about the little details in our lives.

Trust in the Lord to lead you today. He will use you in ways that you may not be aware of, or He may use you in a very clear and practical way to bless the life of someone in need.

Today Is Your Best Day
Because of God's Leading (Part 2)

*"After he has gathered his own flock, he walks ahead of them,
and they follow him because they recognize his voice.
They won't follow a stranger; they will run from him
because they don't recognize his voice."*
JOHN 10:4–5 NLT

"My sheep recognize my voice; I know them, and they follow me."
JOHN 10:27 NLT

God leads us in ways that are unplanned and often unknown by us. We never know exactly all that God has for us in a day. Each day is an adventure in faith as we commit our day into His hands and trust Him to direct our steps in the things that will please Him and bring Him glory.

My wife and I once lived in an apartment complex that was located near my work. Several other people lived in the apartments that we had gotten to know through church or my job. On one particular Sunday, after returning from church, my wife said, "I feel that the Lord wants me to bring a bag of groceries to our neighbor, Jane." (Jane was a single mom with two young daughters who lived two doors down from us.) I could sense that my wife was sharing something that God had put on her heart.

When we entered our apartment she immediately went to the pantry, got a grocery bag, and filled it with food supplies from off the shelves. When she was finished, she picked up the bag and said, "I won't be long," and headed out the front door to our neighbor's apartment. She was gone less then ten minutes, and when she returned I asked her how things went at Jane's.

"It was quite an experience," she answered. "When I got to Jane's, I knocked on the door and waited for a few moments. Everything was quiet. When Jane finally opened the door and saw me holding a bag full of groceries, she became very surprised and curious. I told her that on the way home from church I had sensed the Lord leading me to bring her a bag of groceries. I told her to receive them as a gift from Him. When I handed Jane the grocery bag, she tearfully replied, 'Do you know what I was doing before you knocked on my door? The girls and I were sitting at the dinner table. I had just prayed and thanked the Lord for our lunch, but we had no food on the table, and nothing to eat in the house. I heard your knock just as I had finished praying. The Lord sent you at the perfect time!' "

The Lord will lead you today in His perfect way and wisdom. He may even use you to be an answer to someone's prayer.

Today Is Your Best Day

Because of Spiritual Riches

You know how full of love and kindness
our Lord Jesus Christ was. Though he was very rich,
yet for your sakes he became poor,
so that by his poverty he could make you rich.
2 Corinthians 8:9 NLT

Jesus Christ has truly made you rich—rich in the things that are of the highest value, that are worthy of the loftiest praise, and that will bring you the greatest pleasures. God has made His heavenly riches yours because He is rich in mercy toward you. Spiritual riches mean that God will enrich your life, supply your needs, satisfy your soul, nurture your spirit, build up your faith, increase your strength, fill your heart, and abundantly bless you. He will do this in every way, in all things, and at all times.

Your riches will never fade away, rust away, or be stolen away. You are rich in grace, rich in favor, and rich in blessings. The blessings that are yours in Christ are greater than all material blessings here on earth. God wants you to know the blessings that are yours now, so that you can benefit from them today. Here are some of the rich blessings that are yours:

- *Peace:* You have peace with God (Romans 5:1).
- *Joy:* You can be filled with all joy and peace (Romans 15:13).
- *Love:* His love fills your heart (Romans 5:5).
- *Freedom:* You are freely justified (Romans 3:24).
- *Hope:* You can abound in hope (Romans 15:13).
- *Life:* You are dead to sin and alive to God (Colossians 2:13).
- *Grace:* You are under grace (Romans 6:14).
- *Calling:* You have a divine calling (Ephesians 1:18).
- *Newness:* You are being conformed to Christ's image (Romans 8:29).
- *Change:* You've been given the mind of Christ (1 Corinthians 2:16).
- *Inheritance:* You are a child of God and His heir (Romans 8:16–17).
- *Victory:* You have spiritual victory (1 Corinthians 15:57).
- *Redemption:* You have been redeemed (Galatians 3:13).
- *Enrichment:* You are enriched in everything (1 Corinthians 1:5).

- *Strength:* You can be strengthened by His might (Ephesians 3:16).
- *Wisdom:* You have His wisdom, righteousness, and sanctification (1 Corinthians 1:30).
- *Riches:* You have been given an inheritance (Ephesians 1:11).
- *Comfort:* You are comforted in hard times (2 Corinthians 1:4).
- *Growth:* You can discover new things about God's love (Ephesians 3:18).
- *Authority:* You are seated with Christ (Ephesians 2:6).
- *Fullness:* You can be filled with God's fullness (Ephesians 3:19).
- *Access:* You have access to God (Ephesians 2:18).
- *Triumph:* You can always be triumphant (Romans 5:17).
- *Power:* You have God's power working in you (Ephesians 3:20).
- *Boldness:* You have boldness in prayer (Ephesians 3:12).
- *Gifting:* You have a spiritual gifting (Ephesians 4:7–8).
- *Completeness:* You are complete in Him (Colossians 2:10).

- *Deliverance:* You have been delivered from darkness (Colossians 1:13).
- *Knowledge:* You can be filled with the knowledge of His will (Colossians 2:2–3).
- *Light:* You are a child of the light (1 Thessalonians 5:5).
- *Holiness:* You are cleansed and set apart for God's purposes (Hebrews 10:14).
- *Prosperity:* You can prosper in body, soul, and spirit (3 John 2).
- *Overcoming:* You can overcome because of His greatness in you (1 John 4:4).

Today Is Your Best Day

Because of What Jesus Says

Your words were found, and I ate them, and Your word was to
me the joy and rejoicing of my heart; for I am called by Your
name, O LORD God of hosts.

JEREMIAH 15:16 NKJV

The first time I saw my wife I was attracted to her. We were students in Bible school, and I was introduced to her in the school cafeteria during the lunch hour. After our brief visit I knew that I wanted to talk with her again. I arranged for a triple date with some other friends. The date was a picnic in the country. It turned out to be a big hit, and I knew that I wanted to keep seeing her.

The more I knew her, the more I wanted to know her. In order to find out if she felt the same way about me, I would sometimes ask one of her close friends if she ever said anything about me. Whenever I heard something positive or encouraging it would make my day. My hopes soared, my confidence increased, and my heart grew closer to hers.

Jesus is saying things to you today that will make your

hopes soar, increase your faith, and cause your heart to grow closer to His. Here are some of the things that Jesus is saying to you today (and some of the things He isn't saying).

- He doesn't say: Get away from Me. He says: "Come to Me."

- He doesn't say: What I have to give is not available to you. He says: "Abide in Me."

- He doesn't say: You'll have to make it on your own. He says: "I am your Shepherd."

- He doesn't say: You'll have to figure things out for yourself. He says: "I am the Truth."

- He doesn't say: I never want to see you again. He says: "I am with you always."

- He doesn't say: You'll have to turn around and go back. He says: "Follow Me."

- He doesn't say: I will cut you off from My blessings. He says: "Come to Me and drink."

- He doesn't say: I cannot use you. He says: "I will make you fishers of men."

- He doesn't say: Give Me a good reason to love you. He says: "I love you."

- He doesn't say: You don't fit in My circle. He says: "I have called you friend."

- He doesn't say: You are of no interest to Me. He says: "I have prayed for you."

- He doesn't say: You will not be welcome in heaven. He says: "I go to prepare a place for you."

Today Is Your Best Day

Because of What God Says

I will hear what God the LORD will speak:
for he will speak peace unto his people, and to his saints.
PSALM 85:8 KJV

Some of the greatest blessings that a child receives from his father are the spoken words that assure a child of the father's personal love and care. I will always be grateful for the things my dad spoke into my life. Even though my dad is now in heaven, I still carry the words that his heart spoke to mine.

Today, God is your Father through your personal relationship with His Son, Jesus Christ. You are God's child, and as your Father, God has many things that He wants you to know, to believe, and to hold on to as treasures from Him.

Here are some of the things that His heart speaks (and doesn't speak) to your heart today.

- He doesn't say: I have no interest in you. God says: "I care for you."

- He doesn't say: You will have to fend for yourself. God says: "I will supply all your needs."

- He doesn't say: I love you today, but I can't be sure about tomorrow. God says: "I have loved you with an everlasting love."

- He doesn't say: Don't count on Me. God says: "I will never fail you."

- He doesn't say: You have plenty of reasons to be fearful. God says: "Do not be afraid."

- He doesn't say: There are things in your life that are too big for Me to handle. God says: "Trust Me."

- He doesn't say: Your life is subject to chance and fate. God says: "Your times are in My hands."

- He doesn't say: There are some things that are out of My control. God says: "I rule over all."

- He doesn't say: I am your enemy. God says: "I am for you."

- He doesn't say: I really don't care what happens to you. God says: "When needed, I will discipline you as your loving Father."

- He doesn't say: Sorry, but I am busy right now. God says: "Call upon Me and I will answer you."

- He doesn't say: I can't figure out what to do with you. God says: "I know the plans I have for you."

Today Is Your Best Day

Because of the Will of God

Don't copy the behavior and customs of this world, but let God transform you into a new person by changing the way you think. Then you will know what God wants you to do, and you will know how good and pleasing and perfect his will really is.

ROMANS 12:2 NLT

It can't get any better than being in the will of God for your life. Living in the will of God means that today is your best day. The will of God for you is the right thing, the most fulfilling thing, and the wisest thing you can do. His will is perfectly suited for you. Living in His will brings you the deepest peace, the greatest joy, and the highest purpose you can know. His will keeps you from regrets, from the consequences of foolish choices, and from the lost time of traveling down wrong pathways.

Only those who turn away from the will of God have turned away from the best. Adam's and Eve's worst day was when they followed Satan's will for them instead of God's, and ate the forbidden fruit. Jonah's worst day was when he got out of the will of God, boarding a ship going in the opposite direction of where God had told him to go. The rich ruler, who asked Jesus how he could have eternal life, experienced his worst day when he said "no" to Jesus and "yes" to his riches.

There is nothing bad for you in the will of God. Being in the will of God for your life may mean difficulty, suffering, or persecution, but it will never mean that you could have chosen something better or of higher good. Every day, Jesus lived the best life anyone could ever live, because every day He did the will of His Father. The apostle Paul was a man who was committed to live in the will of God each day. He said that he did the will of God from his heart. He loved the will of God and longed to do the will of God. For Paul, the will of God was not a secondary choice, but the highest choice he could make in life.

One day I purchased something that was out of God's will for me. By reasoning, I tried to persuade myself that I had made the best decision, but I had no sense of God's peace. All my reasons for making the purchase could not restore God's peace to my heart. I wrestled over the issue during the night and into the next morning. Finally, by midmorning, I decided that the peace of God was more important to me than what I had bought. I immediately returned my purchase and spent the rest of the day celebrating the peace of God that had returned to my heart.

Living in the will of God may mean that someone will

misunderstand you, disapprove of what you're doing, pressure you to do what they want, or oppose you in a way that will make your obedience to God difficult. However, this is your best day because you don't have to defend yourself—God is your defender; you don't have to protect yourself—God is your protector; you don't have to look out for yourself—God is your provider. Living in the will of God means that you are living under the approval of God, and His approval is all you really need.

Today Is Your Best Day

Because of Prayer (Part 1)

*Let us therefore come boldly unto the throne of grace,
that we may obtain mercy, and find grace to help
in time of need.*

HEBREWS 4:16 KJV

The benefits of prayer are endless, the effectiveness of prayer is limitless, and the opportunities in prayer are boundless. Today is your best day because of the impact, the influence, and the power of prayer.

There is no wall that can keep prayer out, no policy that can shut prayer out, and no law that can wipe prayer out. Through prayer you can go places you've never been, impact people you've never met, discover things you've never known, open up your heart to joys you've never experienced, and move the hand of God in ways you've never seen.

God, through prayer, invites you to receive of His grace and mercy whenever you are in need. He encourages you to ask, to knock, and to call upon Him so that you may learn His will, know His heart, and receive His answers. Your prayers can have an important part in seeing a lost soul saved, a weak person strengthened, a needy person helped, a weary person encouraged, and a bound person set free.

The opportunities and possibilities of prayer are vast. Think of these examples to build your faith:

- *Abraham's servant* prayed for guidance and found a wife for Isaac (Genesis 24).
- *Moses* prayed and bitter waters turned sweet (Exodus 15:25).
- *Moses* prayed for Miriam's leprosy and saw her healing (Numbers 12:13–15).
- *Gideon* prayed and had God's guidance confirmed to him (Judges 6:36–40).
- *Hannah* prayed and conceived a son (1 Samuel 1:10–17).
- *Samson* prayed and received strength to destroy his enemies (Judges 16:28–30).
- *David* prayed in the time of adversity and God delivered him (Psalm 118:5).
- *Solomon* prayed and God gave him wisdom (1 Kings 3).
- *Elijah* prayed and the weather changed (1 Kings 17:1–7)
- *Daniel* prayed and God revealed things to him (see the book of Daniel).

- *Zacharias* prayed for a child and God gave him a son (Luke 1:13).
- *The disciples* prayed for Peter and God delivered him from prison (Acts 12).
- *Jesus* prayed for His disciples and the Holy Spirit came (John 14:16).

Today Is Your Best Day

Because of Prayer (Part 2)

Don't worry about anything; instead, pray about everything.
Tell God what you need, and thank him for all he has done.
If you do this, you will experience God's peace, which is far more
wonderful than the human mind can understand. His peace will
guard your hearts and minds as you live in Christ Jesus.

PHILIPPIANS 4:6–7 NLT

Why has God called us to prayer? Many reasons have been given, but one that has been a great blessing to me is how prayer allows me to discover something new and very special about God's personal love and care. Through prayer, God has something new for you every day. God has so many creative ways to keep your heart surprised and delighted as He answers your prayers and blesses your life with His very best.

A few months after our marriage, my wife and I were on our way to Mexico to serve as missionaries. En route, we spent three months in Ensenada, a small seacoast city in Baja California. We were there to study the Spanish language with my brother and his wife. They had just completed language school and were also planning on going to Mexico as missionaries.

One morning, about six weeks into our studies, we woke up to discover that two fuses had blown in our fuse box, leaving us without electricity. We also needed to replace our five-gallon jug of drinking water. At that time fuses were ten cents each, and the jug of water was twenty cents. In all, we needed forty cents. Between the four of us we had no money. We looked to the Lord for our need.

"Let's go to the post office," I suggested. "Perhaps some money has come to us in the mail." All four of us piled into our pickup and headed into town. We opened our mailbox with great expectation, but found it empty. We knew that if God was going to meet our need of forty cents that day, it would not be through the mail.

"I think I'll go take a walk on the beach," my brother said, a few moments after our return from town. He was gone about twenty minutes. When he came back to the house we were renting, he stood in the doorway, holding a piece of paper in his hand. Upon closer examination we realized he was holding a five peso bill.

"Where did you get that?" we exclaimed.

"I was walking on the beach and talking to the Lord in prayer, when I noticed something sticking up out of the sand. I walked over and picked it up. It was folded and dirty, and at first I couldn't tell what it was. To my amazement, when I

when an inner voice told me to stop and bend down. As I bent toward the ground I extended my hand in front of me, brushed back some leaves, and there before my eyes was the missing valve.

Today is your best day because God is in every detail, and nothing is too hard for Him.

Today Is Your Best Day

Because of God's Wings

"The LORD repay your work, and a full reward be given you by the LORD God of Israel, under whose wings you have come for refuge."

RUTH 2:12 NKJV

God uses the term "wings" to help you understand more fully what it means to have His presence throughout your day, and His covering over you moment by moment. The Bible speaks about the wings of a mother hen, the wings of an eagle, and the wings (or fringes) of a garment, and applies them to the ways God is working in your life and watching over you. God's wings apply to His care, His protection, His health, His safety, and His strength.

- *As your covering,* God's wings shield you and cast a shadow over you. His shadow is like the welcomed relief provided by a shade tree on a hot summer's day. God's wings shade you from the damaging rays of adversity and from the heat of every trial and calamity.

- *As an expression of His care,* God's wings draw you close to His heart. In His care He knows your every movement, senses your every need, hears your every cry, and feels your every heartbeat.

- *As an expression of His protection,* God's wings shield you from the searching eye of every prey that seeks to devour or destroy you. He is your protector against every scheme of the enemy, against every lie and deception, against every luring temptation, and against every enticement that would try to move you away from His heart.

- *As an expression of His health,* God's wings are an extension of His tender compassion. His purpose is to keep you healthy and strong, well fed and nurtured, vibrant and full of life. When you are weak or ill, He wraps His wings around you as a mother would wrap her child in a blanket. He assures you of His love, draws you close, keeps you warm, feeds you with the food of His faithfulness, renews your vitality, and causes you to grow strong. "But to you who fear My name the Sun of Righteousness shall arise with healing in His wings," says Malachi 4:2 (NKJV).

- *As an expression of His strength,* God's wings carry you to new heights, to new adventures of faith, to new discoveries of His majesty, and to new vistas of grace that your heart can explore and delight in.

Today you are under God's extreme watch-care. He calls you to draw near and trust fully in the covering of His wings. You are the Lord's delight and the apple of His eye. Today is your best day because your life couldn't be in better hands or under better care.

Today Is Your Best Day

Because of Preparation

But now, O Lord, thou art our father;
we are the clay, and thou our potter; and we all are the work of
thy hand.
ISAIAH 64:8 KJV

Like clay in the hands of a skilled craftsman, God is forming you for His purposes, shaping you for His plans, and molding you as a vessel fit for the Master's use. The vessel He is shaping you into will have no errors in its design. Do not think that your vessel needs to be a certain shape or size to be significant.

> *God may shape you into a tiny vessel that can easily be used to pour oil into the wounds of others;*
> *He may shape you as a candle and place you in a dark place to shine for Him;*
> *He may shape you into a cup to bring living water to a thirsty soul;*
> *He may shape you into a handheld basin that can humbly be used to wash a disciple's feet.*

God is using you today and is fulfilling His perfect plan for your life, and at the same time, He is also preparing you for what He has ahead. God is preparing you for a prepared place, a prepared ministry, and for a prepared people that He wants you to reach. God will use various things in your life for His preparation, even the things that are unpleasant:

> *He used the desert to prepare Moses;*
> *He used opposition to prepare Jacob;*
> *He used slavery to prepare Joseph;*
> *He used famine to prepare Gideon;*
> *He used persecution to prepare Paul;*
> *He used isolation to prepare John.*

Nothing about your day is being wasted. You are in God's capable, loving, skillful hands, and you are living under His constant watch-care. He knows how to perfectly prepare you for what He has ahead.

> *He is teaching you so you can respond to His voice and*
> *   learn the importance of quick obedience;*
> *He is testing your faith so you can learn how to trust*
> *   Him completely in the battles of life;*
> *He is disciplining you so you can stand tall as you*
> *   march under His banner;*
> *He is building your character so you can represent Him*
> *   as His witness to a lost and needy world.*

Today Is Your Best Day

Because of Motivation

We know how much God loves us, and we have put our trust in him. God is love, and all who live in love live in God, and God lives in them. And as we live in God, our love grows more perfect.

1 JOHN 4:16–17 NLT

The story is told of a woman who was married to a man who was harsh and cruel. He constantly placed demands upon her. Each day, before the man went to work, he would give his wife a list of jobs that he expected her to do before he returned home. In the evening, the man would go around the house with his list and inspect what his wife had done. If she didn't complete the list or if she did something poorly, he would become angry with her, scold her, and demand she do better the next day. It didn't take long for the woman's heart to be crushed and her love to be quenched.

In time, the woman's cruel husband died. She never thought she could marry anyone again. After some time, the most wonderful man entered her life. He was kind, thoughtful, and understanding. He constantly encouraged her. She was very guarded at first, but his constant love and devotion slowly broke down her walls of resistance. A few years passed, the woman's heart opened up to his love, and they were married. The woman began to live a life that she thought impossible. Each day was filled with happiness.

One day the woman was cleaning out her desk when she came upon an old piece of paper. On it was a list of duties written by her first husband. As she read the list, the woman's heart was overcome with joy. She realized that in her new marriage, she was doing everything that was on that list without being aware of it. Nothing she did seemed like work at all. Everything was motivated by joy and the love she had for her husband, instead of by duty and fear.

The love God has for you and your love for Him work together to make this your best day. There is no higher, better, or richer way to live a day. This relationship is possible because God loved you first. He didn't wait on you to respond to Him before He showed you His loving favor. His love pursued you when your heart was far away from His. God not only loved you first, but He loves you best. You will never know a love as glorious and generous as the love that God has for you.

It is God's love for you that makes you a debtor of His love. Your love debt to God motivates you, not only to love Him in return, but to bring His love to others. Paul tells us to owe no one anything except the debt of love. It is Christ's love that controls you and moves you to respond to Him and to the people He brings into your life. Let all you do today flow out of the joys that come from your love relationship with Him.

Today Is Your Best Day

Because of Change

*"For I am about to do a brand-new thing. See, I have already
begun! Do you not see it? I will make a pathway through the
wilderness for my people to come home. I will create rivers
for them in the desert!"*

ISAIAH 43:19 NLT

God never changes, but He is a changer. Because God
never changes, you can trust His flawless character;
because He is a changer, you can trust His creative
hand. He changes darkness into light, deserts into waterways,
water into wine, mountains into low places, wastelands into
grain fields, death into life, ashes into beauty, mourning into
joy, and rough places into smooth paths.

There is a process for purifying wine that is referred to in
the Old Testament. We are told that wine was poured into a
vessel and then left to sit for a season. During this time the
impurities within the wine would settle to the bottom of the
vessel. After this, the wine was poured from vessel to vessel so
that the purifying process could continue, and the wine could
become more fragrant and sweeter to the taste.

Like the wine, our lives are poured from vessel to vessel. God pours us into His appointed vessels. This pouring often involves times of heart change. This pouring also keeps us from becoming stale and stagnant. When God brings change it means that He is moving us out of something that has been comfortable and into something new that will cause our faith to grow, our hearts to be purified, and our vision to be broadened.

What are the heart changes God is bringing into your life? He may be pouring you into a new relationship, into a new line of work, into a new ministry, or into a new location. He may be bringing a new truth to your heart, allowing you to see a certain circumstance in a new way, imparting a new spiritual gift, opening up a new avenue of obedience, or setting you aside for a time of rest and refreshing.

Whatever vessel God may be using, it will be the best for you and bring His very best to you.

Today Is Your Best Day

Because of Newness

Therefore if any man be in Christ, he is a new creature: old things are passed away; behold, all things are become new.

2 CORINTHIANS 5:17 KJV

Today is your best day because God has exchanged your old way of life for a new way of life. In Jesus, everything in your life experiences a new beginning. Your past sins no longer stand against you, and a holy life is now before you. Your new life means that the way you used to be is not the way you have to be.

Your new life is not based upon your determination, but on God's transformation.

It is not about making resolutions to do better or following certain steps for self-improvement. God didn't try to improve you; rather, He *renewed* you and made you a new creation in Christ. God did not take your old way of life and try to patch it up or build it up. He did something far better. He brought an end to your old way of life by crucifying it on the cross with Christ. Through the cross, God has dealt with everything in your life that was a hindrance to your relationship with Him. "I have been crucified with Christ;" the apostle Paul wrote, "it is no longer I who live, but Christ lives in me; and the life which I now live in the flesh I live by faith in the Son of God, who loved me and gave Himself for me" (Galatians 2:20 NKJV).

Today your old way of life has no claim upon you and no power over you. Your new life is the life of Jesus Christ. The life of Christ in you does not need improvement. It is a resurrected life. Everything about it is good, right, freeing, and loving.

> *Christ's life means His power is your strength;*
> *His will is your purpose;*
> *His mind is your wisdom;*
> *His love is your motivation;*
> *His presence is your joy.*
>
> *In your old way of life everything depended upon you;*
> *in your new way of life everything depends upon Christ.*
> *In your old way of life you were at the center; in your*
> *new way of life Christ is at the center.*
> *In your old way of life you tried to be self-sufficient; in*
> *your new way of life Christ is your sufficiency.*

God's call upon you today is to walk in newness of life, and to put on your new life as you would put on a new garment. "Now you're dressed in a new wardrobe," the apostle Paul said. "Every item of your new way of life is custom-made by the Creator, with his label on it. All the old fashions are now obsolete" (Colossians 3:10 MSG).

Newness of life means that today God wants you to be dressed in His very best.

Today Is Your Best Day

Because of Dependency

"Yes, I am the vine; you are the branches.
Those who remain in me, and I in them, will produce much
fruit. For apart from me you can do nothing."
JOHN 15:5 NLT

As God's child, today is your best day because you are totally and completely dependent upon Him. There is no
way that today could be your best day if you were dependent upon yourself—your finances, friends, talents, abilities, resources, looks, body, personality, will, mind, or emotions. Money
runs out, friends come and go, talents and abilities wear down,
resources diminish, and looks change. Your personality is flawed,
your body is aging, your mind has limitations, and your emotions
rise and fall. God is your only rock, your only security, your only
certainty, and your only hope.

How blessed you are to be dependent upon God today.

His kingdom is unshakable,
His power is unquestionable,

His wisdom is unmistakable,
His love is undeniable.

You are blessed to be dependent upon the One who is perfect, whose ways are past finding out, whose kingdom is without end, whose power is limitless, whose glory is endless, and whose love is boundless.

Dependency upon God means that your life is in the hands of the One who created the heavens, who designed the galaxies, who painted the sunsets, who set the earth in space, and whose hand formed every creature that walks, swims, crawls, runs, or flies.

Dependency upon God means that you have set your heart upon Him and put your faith in Him. God will not fail you.

When you face a problem He will solve it;
When you have a need He will meet it;
When you have a burden He will carry it;
When you face a barrier He will remove it.

Today you are as dependent upon God as your lungs are upon the air, as your body is upon nourishment; as your vision is upon light. God has made everything within you cry out to Him, and as you do, you can be sure that He will answer. Today He says, "Call upon Me. . .and I will show you great and mighty things which you know not."

Today Is Your Best Day

Because of the Cross

Looking unto Jesus, the author and finisher of our faith, who for the joy that was set before Him endured the cross, despising the shame, and has sat down at the right hand of the throne of God.

HEBREWS 12:2 NKJV

Was the crucifixion of Jesus Christ His worst day or His best day? From a human perspective everything about the cross looked like His worst day. His beaten body, the pain of the nails being driven into His hands and feet, the agony of hanging from beams of wood, His blood being poured out upon the ground—all of these point to failure and defeat if we do not understand the reason for His suffering. The events that preceded the cross only heighten the sense of His failure to the onlooker—the betrayal, the false witness brought against Him, the illegal trial, the mockery, the shame, the spitting, the pulling out of His beard, the lashing of His flesh, the crown of thorns.

From a divine perspective and from a believer's perspective, the crucifixion, with all its horror, was Jesus' *best* day. It was His best day because prophetically this truly was the "day that the Lord had made." This was the day the Father had planned when He sent His only begotten Son into the world. All of Jesus' life on earth pointed to this day. This day was known before He was conceived in Mary's womb by the Holy Spirit, for it was at that time that Joseph heard these words, "You shall call His name Jesus, for He will save His people from their sins."

The Bible tells us that Jesus endured the cross, despising its shame, for the joy that He knew would be His. It was Jesus' best day because He came to do the will of God; because He could say, "It is finished"; because He would receive the reward of His suffering; because He destroyed the works of the devil; because He redeemed us back to God; because He glorified His Father.

Jesus' death on the cross has also made it possible for this day to be your best day. He took your sins upon Himself so that you could be forgiven; so that you could receive eternal life; so that you could be justified; so that you could have peace with God; so that you could be His bride; so that you could know Him, love Him, and serve Him; so that you could carry the hope of heaven in your heart today.

Today Is Your Best Day

Because of Your Foundation

*"These words I speak to you are not mere additions to your life,
homeowner improvements to your standard of living. They are
foundation words, words to build a life on. If you work the
words into your life, you are like a smart carpenter who dug
deep and laid the foundation of his house on bedrock.
When the river burst its banks and crashed against the
house, nothing could shake it; it was built to last."*

LUKE 6:47–48 MSG

Today is your best because of the foundation that your
life is being built upon.

I recently watched a documentary about the con-
struction work that is taking place around the San Francisco
Bay area. Many of the large structures that were built over sixty-
five years ago are being reinforced to be able to withstand a
massive earthquake. One of the buildings in need of strength-
ening is the prison on Alcatraz Island. The person in charge of
this project stated that the best way to secure the building is to
anchor it deep into the very rock that it was built upon.

The Bible tells us that one day everything upon this earth will be shaken. This shaking will be more powerful than any known earthquake that has ever been recorded or can even be imagined. When this shaking takes place, the only things that will remain are eternal things. The eternal things that remain are stronger and more secure than the rock upon which Alcatraz stands. Jesus said that the only way a person's life can be secure is to build it upon Him and His words. He is the solid foundation of your faith and the rock upon which you stand.

The Psalms often remind us of the importance of having God as our rock, our refuge, our security, and our strength.

> *When you feel faint or feeble, God is the rock that stands higher than your emotions or inadequacies; When you sense that you are being pulled into a mud pit of despair, only God's hand can lift you out of the mire and place you on the solid ground of His loving care; When you are under attack from the enemy, God is your rock of defense and keeps you in a place where your enemies cannot reach you; When you cry out to God in time of trouble, He will be your rock of deliverance as He answers your prayer and calms your heart.*

What is your heart's response to God today? Let it be one of praise, glory, and thankfulness. Because God is who He is, you can stand sure today without the fear of anything under you slipping away. Hear the words of the psalmist when he proclaims, "The LORD is my rock, my fortress, and my savior; my God is my rock, in whom I find protection. He is my shield, the strength of my salvation, and my stronghold" (Psalm 18:2 NLT).

Today Is Your Best Day

Because You Are Saved (Part 1)

Even when we were dead in sins, hath quickened us together with Christ, (by grace ye are saved;)... For by grace are ye saved through faith; and that not of yourselves: it is the gift of God: Not of works, lest any man should boast.
EPHESIANS 2:5, 8–9 KJV

Think of it. You are saved. You are forgiven. Jesus is your Savior and your life belongs to Him. Your past sins are in the sea of God's forgetfulness (and as Corrie ten Boom has added, "He has put up a sign that says, 'no fishing.' "). You have eternal life, you are on your way to heaven, and you have a God-given purpose here on earth.

The sky may be gray today, but you are saved; someone may have hurt you or let you down, but you are saved; you may be going through a difficult time, but you are saved; the enemy may be attacking you with doubts and fears, but you are saved; you may be tired, alone, or unappreciated, but you are saved. "What we suffer now is nothing," the apostle Paul wrote, "compared to the glory he will give us later" (Romans 8:18 NLT).

Today there are an endless number of reasons why your heart should be rejoicing and thankful that you are saved. If you weren't saved, you would be lost; under guilt and condemnation; without God and without hope in this present evil world; empty inside and without peace; in bondage to the enemy and dead in your trespasses and sins; without any eternal purpose, and no hope of heaven. What could be worse than that?

You are saved!
Saved by God's grace;
Saved because God loves you;
Saved because He sent His only begotten Son;
Saved because Jesus died for you;
Saved because Jesus shed His blood;
Saved because God provided everything that was needed for you to come to Him and receive His loving embrace.

Today you have not only been saved by Him, but you are also being kept by Him, and He will bring you safely home. What could be better than that?

Today Is Your Best Day

Because You Are Saved (Part 2)

I passed on to you what was most important and what had also been passed on to me—that Christ died for our sins, just as the Scriptures said. He was buried, and he was raised from the dead on the third day, as the Scriptures said.

1 CORINTHIANS 15:3–4 NLT

Jesus died and rose for you! Does this not say it all? Jesus' death was in the Father's heart before the world was formed, before a flower bloomed, before a creature moved, before man walked in God's garden, before you took your first breath.

Because of God's grace and mercy toward us, we can look back over our lives at all the wrong we have done—the sins we've committed, the promises we've broken, the evil thoughts we've entertained; our failures, our shortcomings, our inconsistencies, our hypocrisies—and hear our Heavenly Father say to us, "You are forgiven. I have washed you clean, even whiter than snow. My Son's righteousness has become your righteousness because He died and rose for you."

When we look back over our lives at the good things we've tried to do to earn God's favor—the people we've helped, the kind deeds we've done, the nice things we've said, the money we've given, the hard work we've done—we hear our Heavenly Father say to us, "Your righteousness will never be enough to save you or keep you. No amount of work that you do can justify you in My presence. By the righteousness of the law no one can be justified. That is why My Son died and rose for you. By faith alone, His righteousness is now yours."

Does God love you today? Yes, Jesus died and rose for you.
Does God care about you? Yes, Jesus died and rose for you.
Does God provide for you? Yes, Jesus died and rose for you.
Does God forgive you and restore you? Yes, Jesus died
and rose for you.
Does God have a plan for your life? Yes, Jesus died and
rose for you.
Does God have a place for you in heaven? Yes, Jesus died
and rose for you.

Jesus died and rose for you—
If you only knew this one truth, it would be enough.
If you only had this spiritual bread to eat, it would
sustain you.
If you only had this glass of living water to drink, it
would quench your thirst.

If you only could embrace this one aspect of His love, it would bring you comfort.
If you only had this one reality in your soul, it would bring you everlasting joy.

Jesus died and rose for you! Is this not the taproot from which the tree of life grows? Is this not the song of celebration that fills your innermost being? Is this not the headwaters from which the healing fountains flow? Is this not the pen from which all other glorious things are written—justification, sanctification, redemption, and all the other truths of Holy Scripture are yours because Jesus died and rose for you.

You life today is now an all encompassing "yes" because Jesus died and rose for you.

Today Is Your Best Day

Because of Forever

This world is fading away, along with everything it craves.
But if you do the will of God, you will live forever.

1 JOHN 2:17 NLT

Forever is a beautiful word. When our reference point is God and His Kingdom, everything takes on an eternal perspective. Life is filled with meaning and packed with purpose. Those who have this world as their reference point see only those things which are temporary, short-lived, and passing away.

Everything that God is, He is eternally. He is love, and He loves you all the time. He is good, and He is good to you all the time. There are no ups and downs, highs and lows, or comes and goes with God. What He was to you yesterday when He showed you mercy and grace, He will show to you today.

The acceptance you knew when He lifted you out of your sins is the same acceptance that upholds you today. The arms that were once around you to give you assurance embrace you today. All the delights of His presence, all the joys of His face, all the gladness of His heart, rest upon you today.

Here are some reasons why "forever" is such a beautiful word:

- *You can sing and rejoice in the Lord forever.*
- *The God you trust reigns forever.*
- *God will be with you forever.*
- *You will be with the Lord forever.*
- *God will be your God forever.*
- *The One who is in control of your life is King forever.*
- *God's plans and purposes stay firm forever.*
- *God's Word is true forever.*
- *God's goodness and unfailing love will be yours forever.*
- *God knows your name forever.*
- *You will live in the house of the Lord forever.*
- *Your eternal reward will last forever.*
- *Your love relationship with Jesus will go on forever.*

Because God Is with You

"Fear not, for I am with you; be not dismayed, for I am your God. I will strengthen you, yes, I will help you, I will uphold you with My righteous right hand."

ISAIAH 41:10 NKJV

From the Scripture in Isaiah 41:10 there are several important things for you to be reminded of today:

- *Because God is with you, He does not want you to fear.*
- *Because God is with you, He does not want you to be dismayed.*
- *Because God is with you, He will strengthen you.*
- *Because God is with you, He will help you.*
- *Because God is with you, He will uphold you with His righteous right hand.*

Whatever your fears may be today or whoever your enemies are, you have a Friend that sticks closer to you than a brother. Today is your best day because you do not walk through it alone, abandoned, or forsaken. God is with you and He can handle any situation you face, any foe you encounter, any problem you meet, or any conflict you confront. One plus God is definitely a majority!

All of us can experience fear for many reasons. Fear can come when we face a difficult situation, when we step out into something unknown, when we sense our weakness, or when we take our eyes off the Lord, just as Peter did when he began to walk on water. The Bible does not tell us that something is wrong with us if we are fearful, but it does tell us that God doesn't want us to live in fear. Fear can paralyze us and keep us from moving forward in His will and plan for our lives.

God's presence with you is the reason He gives you to not fear. God told Abraham not to fear because He was his shield. God appeared to Isaac and told him not to fear because He would bless him for his father's sake. God told Joshua not to fear because He had given him the land, and that He would be with him as He was with Moses. David said that when he was afraid he learned to trust in the Lord.

Consider this conversation that God and Moses had together (Exodus 33:12–15 NLT):

> Moses said to the LORD, "You have been telling me, 'Take these people up to the Promised Land.' But you haven't told me whom you will send with me. You call

*me by name and tell me I have found favor with you.
Please, if this is really so, show me your intentions so I
will understand you more fully and do exactly what you
want me to do. Besides, don't forget that this nation is
your very own people." And the LORD replied, "I will
personally go with you, Moses. I will give you rest—
everything will be fine for you." Then Moses said, "If
you don't go with us personally, don't let us move a step
from this place."*

Remember, that today God has a *firm* hold upon you. God is not only with you today, but His mighty hand is holding on to you with every step you take.

Today Is Your Best Day

Because of Intercessory Prayer

Therefore He is also able to save to the uttermost those who come to God through Him, since He always lives to make intercession for them.

HEBREWS 7:25 NKJV

How rich you are when someone is praying for you. It has been said that the poorest person is the one who has no one praying for him. You will never have full knowledge of how many times someone has prayed for you, or how often God has prompted someone to pray for you when you were in need. Those prayers have impacted your life at many times and in many ways.

I know a woman who, during the night, was awakened by God to pray for a friend. She didn't know what the need was, but she began to intercede on her friend's behalf. The next day the woman discovered that at the very hour she was praying, her friend was delivered from a very critical situation.

As a young Bible school student I was given an opportunity to minister to a small group of people. The meeting went quite well and when I returned to campus I was feeling pretty good about myself. It was at that moment that God spoke these words to me: "Your success today was not a result of your talent, but a result of someone who was praying for you."

As young missionaries, my brother and I, along with our wives, were traveling across the United States to visit some people we knew before going into Mexico. The trip was made possible when the Lord unexpectedly provided us with a blue pickup truck. While visiting our friends in Minnesota, we were invited to attend a home prayer meeting. During the meeting we shared our story of how God provided our pickup truck, and we also spoke about our plans to enter Mexico within a few days. When we finished, a man responded with great excitement. "For many days," he said, "God has put it on my heart to pray for Don and Roy, a blue pickup truck, and the country of Mexico. Until tonight, that was all I knew, but what a joy it is for me to actually meet the ones I have been interceding for."

Your life has been impacted by prayer. Today is your best day because prayer has made this day possible. I don't know how many people are praying for you today, but I am certain that at least one person is.

As you seek to walk in the calling of a holy life, someone
is praying for you;
As you face temptation, someone is praying for you;

As you seek the Father's will and His glory, someone is praying for you.

That person is Jesus Christ. He is your faithful Advocate and High Priest. He is the One who saves you to the uttermost, and His intercession for you is to the highest degree possible. He will always be interceding on your behalf.

Before the throne of God above
I have a strong and perfect plea.
A great high Priest whose Name is Love
Who ever lives and pleads for me.
My name is graven on His hands,
My name is written on His heart.
I know that while in Heaven He stands
No tongue can bid me thence depart.
—CHARITIE L. BANCROFT, 1863

Today Is Your Best Day

Because God Will Fill Your Greatest Needs and Deepest Desires

How blessed is God! And what a blessing he is!
He's the Father of our Master, Jesus Christ, and takes us to the
high places of blessing in him. Long before he laid down
earth's foundations, he had us in mind,
had settled on us as the focus of his love.
EPHESIANS 1:3–4 MSG

What are your deepest needs and desires? They are not entertainment, wealth, sports, scholastic achievement, popularity, power, or influence. Your greatest needs and desires are matters of your heart and spirit. They are the deepest things within you that cry out for purpose, fulfillment, intimacy, meaning, and love. They are the longings that God has placed within you, and that only He can meet.

Your cries for belonging He alone can answer;
Your search for meaning He alone can fulfill;
Your thirst for fulfillment He alone can quench;
Your longing for intimacy He alone can satisfy.

God, through His Son, has already satisfied your need for redemption, forgiveness, and reconciliation by being your Redeemer.

- He has met your need for righteousness by becoming your righteousness.

- He has met your need to be cared for by caring for you.

- He has met your need for security by holding you secure in His arms.

- He has met your need for companionship by being the God who is there.

- He has met your need for protection by being your Strong Tower and your Hiding Place.

- He has met your need for wholeness by being your Healer.

- He has met your need for peace by being your Shalom.

- He has met your need for identity by being your Heavenly Father.

- He has met your need for guidance and direction by being your Shepherd and Guide.

- He has met your need for self-worth by sending His Son into the world to die for you.

- He has met your need for hope and comfort by being the God of all Hope and Comfort.

- He has met your need for love by being the God who has loved you with an everlasting love.

Today, as you hunger after His bread, remember that God is seeking the hungry; as you long for living waters, remember that He invites the thirsty to drink; as you seek His presence, remember that He bids you to draw near; as you commit to walk in His ways, remember that He is always on the alert, looking for those who are totally committed to Him; as you desire to know His heart, remember that you are the object of His love.

Today Is Your Best Day

And the Future Will Be Even Better

Looking for the blessed hope and glorious appearing
of our great God and Savior Jesus Christ.
TITUS 2:13 NKJV

The subject of the time machine has been a popular theme in science fiction. A common plot describes how someone discovers a way to go back in time to change the outcome of history. Another version of this plot describes how someone discovers a way to see into the future and tries to warn people about some tragic event ahead. Typically, as the story unfolds, few people believe the person's warnings and only a few people are prepared for what is to come.

The world we live in is a very uncertain place. As people look to the future their fears and concerns only deepen as they worry about what will happen and wonder how things will turn out.

Years ago, when John Wooden was coaching the UCLA college basketball team, I became an avid fan. One evening I sat down in front of my television to watch a game between UCLA and a conference rival. The game was close, and as it neared the end the outcome was uncertain. Fans at the stadium were screaming with excitement, tension was everywhere, and nerves were on edge as the game reached the final minute. Yet, in the midst of all that tension, I sat in my living room, cool, calm, and collected. Even though the drama was high, I remained unfazed. How could this be possible? My reason was simple. The game I was watching was a late-night replay. I already knew the final score, and that UCLA had won.

As a believer in Jesus Christ your future outlook is an upward look. You have a hope and a future that is glorious. The Word of God has already declared to you what the future will be and how things will turn out in the end. You can live today in calmness of soul and peace of heart because the final outcome has already been determined by God. You are on the winning side. Jesus Christ will come for you with a shout, with the voice of the archangel, and with the trumpet of God. He will come triumphant, in power, and full of glory. He will establish His reign upon this earth and rule with a scepter of righteousness. His kingdom is an everlasting kingdom and you will be a part of it all.

Today Is Your Best Day

Because of Heaven

For God has reserved a priceless inheritance for his children.
It is kept in heaven for you, pure and undefiled, beyond
the reach of change and decay.
1 PETER 1:4 NLT

I f you are alive on this earth when Jesus Christ returns, you will be caught up to be with Him forever. What a day that will be! If you were to die today, before the Lord returns, this would still be your best day. Your last day upon this earth will be your first day in heaven. The Bible tells us that to be absent from the body is to be present with the Lord. I recently heard a preacher say, "I don't care what method God uses to get me to heaven, just as long as He gets me there."

> *In heaven you will go from a temporary life to a never-ending life; From a world of darkness to a place of everlasting light; From a life of walking by faith to a life of seeing Jesus face-to-face; From a life of knowing in part to a life of knowing even as you are known.*

In heaven all your tears will be wiped away, all your sorrows will vanish from view, all your weaknesses will be swallowed up in His majesty, and all your suffering will give way to eternal shouts of joy.

My dad was raised in an orthodox Jewish home. He first came to know the Lord at the age of forty. He found a Gideon Bible in a Las Vegas hotel room, stole it, read it for three months, and while reading the book of Isaiah, discovered that Jesus was his Messiah. He lived until the age of eighty-nine. Throughout his Christian life he longed to be with Jesus in heaven. When he sent out letters he would often include these words instead of the date: "One day closer to glory!"

I went to visit him during his last few days on earth. The doctor had told my dad he was suffering from an advanced case of leukemia and only had a few days to live. When my dad heard the doctor's report he got all excited. "Really!" he exclaimed, "you mean I get to go be with Jesus?" My dad began telling people who visited him, "Before you go, let me give you my new address."

Just before my dad passed into a state where he could no longer communicate, a young couple came to his bedside. The young man was quiet and his wife was in tears (my dad had recently led her to Christ). My dad immediately reached out his hand to her and said, "No tears. This is what it's all about. We serve the Lord here on earth for a few years and then we get to be with Him in heaven."

When my dad finally passed out of this life and into the realities of heaven, all of us who had gathered at his bedside gave out a shout of joy in celebration of his homecoming. We all knew that he had arrived at the place where he always wanted to be.

This is the hope all believers in Jesus have. This is the hope that makes every day your best day!